DAILY PERSEVERANCE

JJ MAZZO
USA Today Bestselling Author

DAILY PERSEVERANCE

365 DAYS TO STRENGTHEN YOUR MIND, FAITH, AND LEADERSHIP

WILEY

Published by John Wiley & Sons, Inc., Hoboken, New Jersey.

Library of Congress Cataloging-in-Publication Data:

Names: Mazzo, J J author
Title: Daily perseverance : 365 days to strengthen your mind, faith, and leadership / JJ Mazzo.
Description: Hoboken, NJ : Wiley, 2026. | Includes bibliographical references.
Identifiers: LCCN 2026019569 (print) | LCCN 2026019570 (ebook) | ISBN 9781394444434 hardback | ISBN 9781394444458 adobe pdf | ISBN 9781394444441 epub
Subjects: LCSH: Perseverance (Ethics)—Biblical teaching | LCGFT: Devotional literature
Classification: LCC BV4647.P45 M48 2026 (print) | LCC BV4647.P45 (ebook)
LC record available at https://lccn.loc.gov/2026019569
LC ebook record available at https://lccn.loc.gov/2026019570

COVER DESIGN: WILEY/PAUL MCCARTHY
COVER ART: EKY CHAN/ADOBE STOCK PHOTOS

This book is dedicated to Jesus and my girls,
Kimberly, Brooklyn, and London.

Introduction

In my *USA Today* best seller, *Perseverance Principles*, I walked you through my journey from a troubled childhood, instability, and brushes with the law to becoming a successful businessman, loving husband, and father, fortified by my faith in a Christ-centered life. I wanted to share with you proven perseverance strategies and a winning mindset built on core principles that are easy for you to incorporate in your life, too.

As I wrote that book, it became apparent to me that what I could teach you could be augmented by small, ongoing reminders of what it takes to continue down a positive path every day. I began texting these reminders to my clients, team members, friends, and others whom I knew could benefit from inspirational quick hits. I got so much positive feedback that I decided to expand on these thoughts and share them with more people and new audiences.

Daily Perseverance is the result of those efforts. This book builds on *Perseverance Principles*, and the passages on these pages further explore themes of perseverance, adversity, consistency, confidence, wealth, questions, and reflections. I've augmented them with Biblical passages to reaffirm my strong faith in God and prove how we can tap into our spiritual being to achieve peace, happiness, clarity, and prosperity in our lives.

How to Use This Book

People incorporate meaning and value in different ways with a book like this. Rather than listing a lengthy table of contents, I suggest you take a different approach to using this book.

Daily Perseverance is divided into 52 weekly groups of thoughts, scripture, and anchor thoughts that flow into many parts of your life. Each week includes an entry for seven intentional categories:

Staying the Course to strengthen your resolve to keep moving forward—especially when quitting feels easier

Strength Through the Struggle, which teaches you how to face adversity without letting it define or defeat you

Winning the Ordinary Days to help you discover how small, faithful actions build real momentum over time

Unshakable Confidence that teaches you how to build confidence that doesn't depend on circumstances or outcomes

Building a Life That Lasts that addresses themes of legacy in how you see your work, resources, and influence as tools for purpose—not pressure

Asking the Right Questions as a way to slow down, listen, and realign with what truly matters

What This Week Changed in Me is designed to help you reflect on and capture growth you might have overlooked this week, and to prepare your heart for the week ahead

Many people can start their self-discovery journey in Week 1 at any time of year. You can read one entry each day for an ongoing dose of wisdom to incorporate into your day.

Other people need support in specific areas of their lives. For those people, I suggest you identify the one or two areas you need help with most and intensify your learning by reading several passages in a category in one or two sittings, without being bound by a weekly format.

How you read and add these insights to your life is up to you. I hope it is both a starting point that helps you dig deeper into various areas of your life and an endpoint that leads you to the peace and happiness you deserve.

Week 1

Staying the Course

Refusing to Quit

Some weeks don't start with energy.

They start with weight.

Responsibilities are already waiting. Expectations are already loud. And before you've done anything wrong, the pressure is already present.

Perseverance isn't about intensity—it's about refusal. Refusing to quit. Refusing to drift. Refusing to let a hard moment talk you out of a long-term calling. You don't need to win today.

You just need to stay.

"And let us not be weary in well doing."

—Galatians 6:9 (KJV)

Today's Anchor: Staying the course is a decision you make before the pressure shows up.

Strength Through the Struggle

Stop Feeding Negative Thoughts

Doubt and fear often creep into our lives when the future is uncertain. Our mind tries to protect us from uncertainty by default, but in some cases, that can inadvertently sabotage our dreams.

Focus on habits and routines that have molded you thus far and find ways to expand and refine them to allow for maximum growth going forward.

As you grow this way, you will continue to grow closer to God and what He intended you to be.

> *"Casting down imaginations, and every high thing that exalteth itself against the knowledge of God, and bringing into captivity every thought to the obedience of Christ;"*
>
> *—2 Corinthians 10:5 (KJV)*

Today's Anchor: Replace a passing thought before it becomes a permanent belief.

Winning the Ordinary Days

Keeping Your Best Habits in Place

When you grow, you will often remove habits that no longer serve you well and replace them with more effective habits that do.

The challenge for many people is deciding which habits still positively affect them versus those that must be cut loose.

Keeping old habits in place buys you time to try new things, but you don't need to stack new habits until they have been vetted and are worthy of becoming part of your daily routines.

> *"Therefore, my beloved brethren, be ye stedfast, unmoveable, always abounding in the work of the Lord, forasmuch as ye know that your labour is not in vain in the Lord."*
>
> *—1 Corinthians 15:58 (KJV)*

Today's Anchor: Your best habits are the foundation, and you must protect them like your goals.

Unshakable Confidence

Boxing in Negativity

Research has often verified that we have a negative bias in our way of thinking. It is usually one of our first reactions to anything new and is part of a bigger defense mechanism our brain uses to protect us from the unknown.

Unfortunately, this negativity bias can continue long past its useful help to us. Many people don't know how to turn it off when it gets in the way of doing new things or taking reasonable chances to advance their lives.

You should listen to both sides of your brain as it steers your life in the right direction. Boxing in negativity and not allowing it to run unchecked must be a conscious effort on your part. Flooding your thoughts with gratitude, perspective, and positivity is one of the most effective ways to do it.

> *"Finally, brethren, whatsoever things are true, whatsoever things are honest, whatsoever things are just, whatsoever things are pure, whatsoever things are lovely, whatsoever things are of good report; if there be any virtue, and if there be any praise, think on these things."*
>
> *—Philippians 4:8 (KJV)*

Today's Anchor: Give negativity less room by controlling what you allow to live in your mind today.

Building a Life That Lasts

Leaving Your Debts Behind

What do you need to leave behind in order to succeed?

Some things add to your bottom line and others cost you far beyond dollars and cents. Despite this negative line item on your personal balance sheet, many of you choose to carry them anyway.

If you have reservations about cancelling these debts, know that you can't fully understand the impact a lighter load on you will have until you actually do it. You must have the courage and the endurance to lighten your load now for the amazing journey that waits for you in the future.

"Owe no man any thing, but to love one another."

—Romans 13:8 (KJV)

Today's Anchor: Freedom is built one disciplined decision at a time.

Asking the Right Questions

What Is Your Equation for Life?

Do you have a simple formula you call on often to keep you on track? What is your equation for life?

The equation I use is simple. Focus + Plan + Execution × Discipline = Results.

Can you point to a small group of words to clearly define the results you want to achieve? What are the words and thoughts behind them that bring the most meaning and clarity to your life?

For me, focus, having a plan, executing it, and supercharging it with the force multiplier of discipline for consistency drives me to incredible results.

Live with your equation and revisit the variables that are a part of it often. Change those variables as the equation of your life changes. This part is critical to the "math" of your life.

> *"For what is a man profited, if he shall gain the whole world, and lose his own soul?"*
>
> *—Matthew 16:26 (KJV)*

Today's Anchor: If your inputs don't match the life you want, it's time to change the formula.

What This Week Changed in Me

Are You Holding Back?

What areas of genius have you been holding back out of fear or discomfort? Is it fear of failure, and lack of trust in your process, or a lack of commitment?

Unless you can dive into something with your full heart, even when you don't know all the variables and outcomes, you're avoiding the challenge in front of you for a reason. Those reasons are what separate us from our success.

Can you identify what you need to do that's unrequired and uncomfortable? Can you accept those challenges? Until you do, you are undermining your chances for growth and success.

"For God hath not given us the spirit of fear."

—2 Timothy 1:7 (KJV)

Today's Anchor: The version of you you're praying for is on the other side of one courageous move today.

Weekly Reflection:

____

____

____

____

____

____

Week 2

Staying the Course

Time Discipline

When distractions and inevitable confusion follow, stay focused on the discipline you have created.

If you don't have enough discipline in your life, start small and create a nonnegotiable approach in one part of your life that will move you in the direction you want to go.

Saying no more often and protecting your time is a powerful tool to avoid distractions and confusion that can be otherwise overwhelming.

> *"See then that ye walk circumspectly, not as fools, but as wise . . ."*
>
> —*Ephesians 5:15–16 (KJV)*

Today's Anchor: Time is your most honest scoreboard and you should spend it like a leader, not a victim.

Strength Through the Struggle

Boundaries Are Important

Do you know the boundaries that you should use to guide your life? What things must you avoid to stay on track and what is important to remain focused on where you want to go?

When you keep out things that don't serve you, it creates a natural flow allowing endless blessings to enter your life. This can only happen if you're intentional and remain in charge of the important boundaries you have established.

"Keep thy heart with all diligence."

—Proverbs 4:23 (KJV)

Today's Anchor: Boundaries aren't walls. They're guardrails that keep you headed where you said you are going.

Winning the Ordinary Days

The Importance of Preparation

Preparation takes much of the guesswork out of challenges and action items. When you take adequate time to prepare, it's an indicator that something is important to you. If you just wing it, that may be a clue that what you're engaged in doing may not be important overall.

When you're facing a deadline, ask yourself if you're committed to do the important work beforehand to give yourself the best chance at a positive outcome.

Doing so gives you the gift of removing anxiety and last minute concerns.

"The horse is prepared against the day of battle."

—Proverbs 21:31 (KJV)

Today's Anchor: Preparation is confidence in motion and means you should get ready before you feel ready.

Unshakable Confidence

Listening to Your Internal Voice

Is the little voice in your head a good friend or a challenging foe? It depends on how you listen to it. You must also challenge it when you don't like what you're hearing. Be sure to ask the right questions and weed out negative self-talk that undermines you.

Create a voice that is guided by love, instead of one that has been corrupted by resentment and ego. Keep it in check and you will be guided to your intended result.

> *"My sheep hear my voice, and I know them, and they follow me."*
>
> —*John 10:27 (KJV)*

Today's Anchor: The right voice is usually the quiet one. Slow down long enough to hear it.

Building a Life That Lasts

We Are the Sum of Our Experiences

Experiences are the gift of this life that many of us overlook. We become wrapped up in our daily routines forgetting to pause and savor what God has given us.

It's good to be productive, but it's even better when you can take a moment, reflect on what you've been through, and take away as much meaning as possible.

Enjoy the process and the outcomes. Practice gratitude even when things don't go your way. Your life will not be perfect, but you can derive important lessons from all experiences to build on for the future.

"And we know that all things work together for good to them . . ."

—Romans 8:28 (KJV)

Today's Anchor: God doesn't waste seasons. He uses them to shape you for what's next.

Asking the Right Questions

The Right Solutions Take Time

At times, we are tempted to put a bandage on a problem and hope that it works out. It takes time to search for and implement effective solutions that provide actual value.

When you face a challenging problem, do you take time to sit in your silent thoughts and search for the solution that will bring relief? You may be fooled by the temporary out of convenience but look for the long-term solution that will resolve the issue.

It's valuable to ask, "Am I trying to rush that actually needs more patience, prayer, or perspective?"

> *"But let patience have her perfect work, that ye may be perfect . . ."*
>
> —*James 1:4 (KJV)*

Today's Anchor: Don't rush what needs to be refined because good answers require endurance.

What This Week Changed in Me

Responding to Tough Situations

Have you been responding to tough situations with a version that served you well in the past but doesn't serve you well now?

How often do you think about how to make yourself better by working hard to move past older versions of who you were? It's easy to default what may have worked for us in the past out of comfort and what we already know.

But we are also programmed for growth and seeking new and better ways to go through life. It's up to us to look forward with courage as new challenges come our way.

What do you need to do to continually work this part of your life to make it stronger?

> *"Wherefore, my beloved brethren, let every man be swift to hear, slow to speak, slow to wrath."*
>
> *—James 1:19 (KJV)*

Today's Anchor: Intentionally choose your response before emotions choose for you.

Weekly Reflection:

____

____

____

____

____

____

Week 3

Staying the Course

Patience Must Be Combined with Action

It is difficult to work toward a goal and not see the desired results in the time frame you want. Patience is challenging, especially when outside forces pressure you to get results. As pressure mounts, you may pull back and become scared that deciding to act will only make things worse.

There can be no solutions without taking action. Even when your actions fall short, you learn from your experience, dust yourself off, and take another run at the problem at hand. But this time, you'll be armed with more experience, which may tip the outcome in your favor.

> *"Commit thy works unto the LORD, and thy thoughts shall be established."*
>
> *—Proverbs 16:3 (KJV)*

Today's Anchor: Patience isn't passive. It's an opportunity to seek the right path while you wait.

Strength Through the Struggle

Don't Ignore Hard Things

Until you turn your attention to difficult challenges, they will continue to undermine you. Looking the other way is a poor approach to living your best life. Instead, you must be aggressive on the things that are causing you the most pain. Make it a habit to meet these problems head on so it becomes second nature to you.

As your confidence grows, you will look for bigger mountains to climb instead of seeking the path where most other people live.

"Have not I commanded thee? Be strong and of a good courage."

—Joshua 1:9 (KJV)

Today's Anchor: The thing you keep avoiding is the thing that keeps owning you.

Winning the Ordinary Days

Habits Build Important Foundations

Consistent habits, faithfully put into action, build important foundations over time.

Foundations are the rock-solid thoughts, processes, strategies, and standards we put in place to serve us best. But if we don't consistently follow these foundations through consistent efforts, the foundations will crumble.

We must decide if the habits we engage in now best serve our goals. Are they worthy of our continued time and effort? Ask this question as one of the first steps in building your best foundation.

> *"Therefore whosoever heareth these sayings of mine, and doeth them, I will liken him unto a wise man, which built his house upon a rock."*
>
> *—Matthew 7:24 (KJV)*

Today's Anchor: The life you want is built by purposely stacking small steps over time.

Unshakable Confidence

Having Faith Creates Discipline

Having faith is part of the necessary discipline required to do hard things. Faith is often tested, but to overcome negative biases, we must continually discipline our thoughts, even if it feels uncomfortable.

Use faith to aim your actions daily. Faith and discipline are the most direct ways to get to where you want to go.

Faith looks to the future, and being disciplined is the fuel we need to get us there.

> *"Now faith is the substance of things hoped for, the evidence of things not seen."*
>
> *—Hebrews 11:1 (KJV)*

Today's Anchor: Faith is the fuel, discipline is the vehicle, and you must use both to move forward.

Building a Life That Lasts

Focusing on Peace

The more we focus on peace the less distractions vie for our attention. When we know that peace is a goal, we can rid anything that disrupts that process. Ultimately we can make negativity fade to the background when focused on the right things.

Deciding what is relevant makes it easier to take the actions that serve our best interests.

Take stock of your mindset and adjust your focus to actions that lead you to that peace.

"Peace I leave with you, my peace I give unto you."

—John 14:27 (KJV)

Today's Anchor: Peace is the presence of trust in the middle of your problems.

Asking the Right Questions

What Parts of You Are Hidden?

What part of ourselves have we hidden from plain sight due to fear of judgment?

Do these false identities serve you well? Chances are they do not and were probably born out a compromise you made with yourself to travel down an easier path.

Are you relying on old falsehoods about yourself that no longer serve you?

If you have the courage to answer these questions, you will be able to redirect your energy to where it should be instead of where others think you should be.

"Search me, O God, and know my heart."

—Psalm 139:23 (KJV)

Today's Anchor: Healing starts when honesty shows up.

What This Week Changed in Me

Stay Focused on the Human Factor

When we're motivated, energized, and focused on our goals, we bulldoze others in our efforts. Often these are the people we care about the most, and they suffer because of our lack of awareness.

In the end, we must also remember that those people have their own goals, dreams, and desires. They are no less or more worthy than ours, just chosen differently by God for His purpose.

> *"And the second is like, namely this, Thou shalt love thy neighbour as thyself."*
>
> *—Mark 12:31 (KJV)*

Today's Anchor: People are never the interruption; they're the assignment.

Weekly Reflection:

____

____

____

____

____

____

Week 4

Staying the Course

Acceptance Is Healing

Losing those we love and care about is a part of life, but often we choose to delay accepting the loss of those we care about.

When it happens we want to give up on things important and rely on sadness to carry us. Grief is an important part of healing; however, it is not meant to be a permanent part of life. As difficult and unique as grief is, we must process it and not fall into an endless spiral of depression.

Sadness that turns to acceptance is healing. Acceptance enables us to rediscover joy, which is more powerful than sadness when we give it the opportunity to reenter our lives.

"The LORD is nigh unto them that are of a broken heart."

—Psalm 34:18 (KJV)

Today's Anchor: Acceptance doesn't excuse what happened. It releases you from living trapped in the past.

Strength Through the Struggle

Leadership and Adversity

Before adversity strikes, and when it does, having the right leaders in the right seats is everything. You must be clear on your role at the top of an organization leading a group of others to support your overall mission.

Understand that each of us has unique abilities and that anything can be accomplished when we work in unison. However, failure is more likely to occur if the right person is doing the wrong task.

When adversity strikes, as a leader you may be unable to avoid disappointments and setbacks, but with the right leadership, you will minimize them.

> *"Feed the flock of God which is among you, taking the oversight thereof, not by constraint, but willingly; not for filthy lucre, but of a ready mind; Neither as being lords over God's heritage, but being ensamples to the flock."*
>
> *—1 Peter 5:2–3 (KJV)*

Today's Anchor: Adversity reveals leadership.

Winning the Ordinary Days

The Limitations of Instant Gratification

We have entered an era of instant gratification. From Amazon to the microwave, we have been conditioned for impatience.

The truth is that meaningful processes and outcomes take time. Planting seeds today and expecting fruit tomorrow is unreasonable. Many things require ongoing attention, effort, and consistency over extended periods to produce meaningful results.

People who focus on short-term payoffs never reach the destination meant for them. As a result, they lead lesser lives than those who persevere and end up with a larger harvest than they ever imagined.

> *"Now no chastening for the present seemeth to be joyous, but grievous."*
>
> —*Hebrews 12:11 (KJV)*

Today's Anchor: Short-term comfort will steal long-term calling, so choose wisely.

Unshakable Confidence

Maintaining the Right Priorities

Protecting your priorities at all costs is critical for success. When you feel that your priorities are negotiable, you need to rethink what they are. Those with clear and valuable meaning will withstand this scrutiny. Those that you are less passionate about must be cut loose to make room for new priorities.

This is not a betrayal of your thought process. It is necessary growth. You have the right to change your mind as you grow and learn new things about your world. Bring them to the forefront to remind you of your purpose and where to continue focusing your efforts.

"But seek ye first the kingdom of God, and his righteousness."

—Matthew 6:33 (KJV)

Today's Anchor: Be sure your "first" is worthy because what you put first gets your best effort.

Building a Life That Lasts

Opportunities Are Wealth

Too often, we measure success by how much money we have in the bank, the size of our homes, or the cars we drive. What we fail to realize is many other forms of wealth are just as valuable as money. Creating opportunities is one of the most valuable among these alternate forms.

The best way to create opportunities is by serving others as much as we serve ourselves. When we freely give our time, advice, and other resources at our disposal, we make important connections. Through these connections, we gain the opportunity to learn, grow, share, and help others. Eventually, these investments come back to us through greater trust, an expanding network of others, and a greater awareness of God's grace.

> *"And whatsoever ye do, do it heartily, as to the Lord, and not unto men."*
>
> *—Colossians 3:23 (KJV)*

Today's Anchor: Opportunity is often a path to your breakthrough.

Asking the Right Questions

What Are Your Anchors of Peace?

In turbulent times, do you know what your anchors of peace are? What are the things that provide you with a safe harbor until the storms have passed? Who are the people in your life that keep you from drifting too far away from the person you want to be?

When you are untethered from these anchors, it's more likely you'll have to deal with negative bias directed at you, and intrusive thoughts you generate on your own. If you don't have a safe place until these things pass, you'll miss out on the joy and peace you deserve.

Find that safe haven and keep it close to you.

> *"Thou wilt keep him in perfect peace, whose mind is stayed on thee."*
>
> *—Isaiah 26:3 (KJV)*

Today's Anchor: Lock into what keeps you grounded because your anchors decide the level of stability.

What This Week Changed in Me

Start Each Day with Gratitude

Starting each day with gratitude changes the course of your mind for the remainder of it.

Let gratitude for one part of your life seamlessly flow to another until you can no longer think of anymore. Dig deep into the small things that we might not notice naturally but that mean so much to us. Remind yourself of the blessings you have been given, and, most importantly, share as many of them with others as often as you can.

Our lives are so much better when we focus on gratitude for others, instead of selfishly focusing on ourselves.

"In every thing give thanks."

—1 Thessalonians 5:18 (KJV)

Today's Anchor: Gratitude resets your perspective. Make it the priority.

Weekly Reflection:

____

____

____

____

____

____

Week 5

Staying the Course

Stay Close to Your Beliefs and Values

As you move through life, you will be tested in many ways. There will be times when you may have doubts about what you believe and value. Some of that is healthy for continued growth, but this must be blended with those things that are nonnegotiable as you decide your path going forward.

As we persevere and remain consistent, we don't need to spend much time thinking about our past, other than to remind us of who we were and how much we have grown.

Instead, we should focus on our faith and the belief that God will provide us with a clear way forward if we choose to take it.

"Trust in the LORD with all thine heart."

—Proverbs 3:5–6 (KJV)

Today's Anchor: Values are more than just words you speak; they're decisions you make under pressure.

Strength Through the Struggle

Adversity Often Disguises Opportunity

Challenges and adversity don't define us but how we respond to them does.

They are often disguised as opportunities when we figure out the right way to reframe them.

These opportunities create growth, finding new levels of perseverance or closing doors to one thing so that we can walk through thc doors of even better ones.

If we ignore all the positives, we'll be miserable, falling into pits of despair, self-pity, or blame. Instead, if we accept that we are imperfect and allow ourselves forgiveness and grace, adversity shrinks, and we are in a better place to pursue challenges with a higher degree of grace.

> *"My brethren, count it all joy when ye fall into divers temptations."*
>
> *—James 1:2–3 (KJV)*

Today's Anchor: Reframe the struggle to look for opportunities inside what you're walking through.

Winning the Ordinary Days

Keep Looking for Opportunities

Unique opportunities are plentiful but taking advantage of them is not. Why do so many miss what's in front of them while looking for what's next?

Instead of making excuses, keep your eyes open for unique opportunities each day and act on them. Start with the obvious opportunities that are in front of you to build momentum.

Find the things that require hard work. Those are the challenges that will grow you the most. Don't coast. Instead, consistently take action to make the most of great opportunities that have been placed in your path.

> *"As we have therefore opportunity, let us do good unto all men, especially unto them who are of the household of faith."*
>
> *—Galatians 6:10 (KJV)*

Today's Anchor: God often hides open doors inside ordinary moments.

Unshakable Confidence

Responding Versus Reacting

When we are passionate about what we do or who we are serving and things don't go as planned, it's our tendency to react.

A better way to approach setbacks or deviations from what we want is to pause and decipher what is really happening, then respond with intention over our emotions to give us the best chance at getting the response we want.

"A soft answer turneth away wrath."

—Proverbs 15:1 (KJV)

Today's Anchor: A calm response is a power move. Pause and think before you speak.

Building a Life That Lasts

Kindness Is a Form of Wealth

When you are generous with your abundant life, it's important to share it with others, early and often.

People may be suspicious of your kindness at first. Wealth shared too quickly and easily is misinterpreted and those who receive it may think about returning it to you.

Do not be dissuaded by this. Simply enter into a giving relationship with positive intention, stay true to your beliefs, and watch how the relationship grows and expands over time.

Be genuine in letting those people know your intentions are honest and noble. Given time, your track record will speak for you and result in more productive and happy relationships than those hobbled by misplaced skepticism.

"The liberal soul shall be made fat."

—Proverbs 11:25 (KJV)

Today's Anchor: Kindness compounds and comes back to you in ways you can't predict.

Asking the Right Questions

Who Are You Surrounding Yourself With?

How often do you scrutinize the people you closely associate with? Can you do this objectively, weighing the good and the bad of those relationships? Do you set aside small lapses in judgment because you have also had those as well?

You don't need to abandon those who are not aligned with you, but can you make the difficult choice of keeping these people at arm's length when they are not unified with what you want to accomplish.

> *"He that walketh with wise men shall be wise."*
>
> *—Proverbs 13:20 (KJV)*

Today's Anchor: Your circle is your ceiling. Choose people who improve you.

What This Week Changed in Me

Are You Protecting Your Mind?

How vigilant are you when it comes to the types of thoughts you allow to enter your mind? If you allow negativity and people who add no value to your life influence you, it's not unreasonable to expect they will push more positive thoughts out of the way.

Be careful what you absorb every day. Do not fall into a pattern of accepting poor attitudes and negativity to penetrate your path. If you don't like what you're hearing, it's time to make changes to adjust who and what influences you.

> *"And be not conformed to this world: but be ye transformed by the renewing of your mind."*
>
> *—Romans 12:2 (KJV)*

Today's Anchor: Guard what you consume to win on the battlefield of your mind.

Weekly Reflection:

____

____

____

____

____

____

Week 6

Staying the Course

The Importance of Picking Yourself Up

We have all heard variations of "It's not how many times you fall down that matters but how many times you get up."

Don't get stuck being down and waiting for others to come along and pick you up.

You are in charge of when and how you get back up.

Get up as quickly as you can. Perseverance is easier when you stand upright. You've done it many times before and there's no reason why you can't do it again.

> *"Rejoice not against me, O mine enemy: when I fall, I shall arise."*
>
> *—Micah 7:8 (KJV)*

Today's Anchor: Falling isn't failure, but staying down is. Get up and get moving.

Strength Through the Struggle

Fighting Discouragement

Our lives are filled with discouragement. We can't help feeling discouraged when setbacks occur, but the key to minimizing this feeling is to avoid lingering in a bad place.

Keep this time frame as short as possible. Learn not to take setbacks personally. Understand they are part of everything worthy you undertake.

Next, flow as much gratitude as possible into your life. Gratitude is a powerful emotion that replaces discouragement with an uplifting mindset that forces us to give thanks for all we have.

If you have a choice, that choice is easy.

> *"Why art thou cast down, O my soul? and why art thou disquieted within me? hope thou in God: for I shall yet praise him, who is the health of my countenance, and my God."*
>
> *—Psalm 42:11 (KJV)*

Today's Anchor: Discouragement is real, but it doesn't get to drive your life unless you allow it to do so.

Winning the Ordinary Days

Be Relentless

Always be relentless. You will fail sometimes and you'll enjoy many successes but you must never be complacent. Complacency is a sign of mediocrity and an acceptance of being average. You were born for something great.

Always move forward in the relentless pursuit of your goals. You will discover that in those moments you are about to quit is when breakthroughs happen.

Let others get complacent and give up, not you, not today.

"For which cause we faint not."

—2 Corinthians 4:16 (KJV)

Today's Anchor: Relentless doesn't mean loud, it means being consistent, even when nobody applauds.

Unshakable Confidence

The Importance of Active Listening

Listening with intention and responding with compassion must be a priority. When we do this, we act quicker because we're more engaged. When we actively engage, there is less overthinking.

When we don't pay attention to the here and now, we stumble, and that leads to miscommunication. We don't wind up with the answers we need that enable us to be decisive going forward.

"He that answereth a matter before he heareth it, it is folly . . ."

—Proverbs 18:13 (KJV)

Today's Anchor: Listen more to understand and less to reply; wisdom shows up when you engage the right way.

Building a Life That Lasts

Knowledge Is the Key

To build lasting wealth, you must keep investing in your education. Stay current with changing conditions and be creative to give you an edge over your competitors.

Also revisit and reflect on what you've already learned. Often answers are buried in those lessons that you may have missed. And some things that weren't as important before may be important now.

When the excitement of learning something new takes root, and you combine it with a fresh take on lessons already learned, you will gain wisdom to become a more formidable force.

"The heart of the prudent getteth knowledge."

—Proverbs 18:15 (KJV)

Today's Anchor: What you learn today becomes what you earn tomorrow.

Asking the Right Questions

Can You Sift Through the Chaos?

Do you know how to sift through all the chaos that threatens to derail you? Do you know where to find the tools you need to remain focused and not overwhelmed?

These are not easy questions to answer. Until you figure out how to answer and implement them, you will struggle. However, asking more questions and finding their answers will guide you from chaos to calm.

"For God is not the author of confusion, but of peace."

—1 Corinthians 14:33 (KJV)

Today's Anchor: Chaos is a distraction so it's critical to filter for truth before you can move with clarity.

What This Week Changed in Me

The Challenge of Authenticity

Being authentic to yourself is easier said than done. We are the product of so many people who have deterred us from being our true selves that sometimes we shy away from the importance of authenticity.

Conforming to things we don't fully believe is sometimes a thought process to protect us from the world. We forget that God intended us to be just how we are and to live our purpose according to His will. When we don't honor that, we suffer.

Be authentic in how you live your life and encourage others to do the same, free from judgment.

> *"Behold, thou desirest truth in the inward parts."*
>
> *—Psalm 51:6 (KJV)*

Today's Anchor: Authenticity costs comfort, but it buys freedom.

Weekly Reflection:

____

____

____

____

____

____

Week 7

Staying the Course

Changing Your Approach

When you do something over and over and expect different results, you're stuck.

If you don't change your approach and make corrections in your behavior or the behavior of others, circumstances often come along to make those changes for you. This robs you of control and can make you veer off course, leading to delays and frustration.

Avoiding changes doesn't mean they won't happen. They will whether you like it or not. Choose to be actively involved in those changes and steer your efforts to the outcomes you want.

> *"And not only so, but we glory in tribulations also: knowing that tribulation worketh patience; And patience, experience; and experience, hope:"*
>
> —*Romans 5:3–4 (KJV)*

Today's Anchor: If the results don't change, the approach must. Learn to adjust without abandoning the mission.

Strength Through the Struggle

Frustrations Are Inevitable

Life is full of people and situations that will frustrate us. We can't avoid them but we can decide how to respond to them. Our responses dictate if they will continue or evaporate into that which no longer worries or concerns us.

Simply put, what we focus on expands. When we are grounded by who we are and who we want to be versus that which stands in our way, we are better able to dictate how we respond and for how long.

Do this and your accomplishments, and not your frustrations, will define who you are.

"Be not hasty in thy spirit to be angry."

—Ecclesiastes 7:9 (KJV)

Today's Anchor: Frustration is a signal you should use to reset instead of simply reacting.

Winning the Ordinary Days

Mastery Matters

Mastery of tasks that are basic or complicated is essential for success. You must pay attention to details, develop optimal processes, and repeat them until it is the only way you know how to operate.

Consistency is a stepping stone to mastery. When we practice mastery as a habit, in time, anything is possible.

> *"And whatsoever ye do in word or deed, do all in the name of the Lord Jesus, giving thanks to God and the Father by him."*
>
> —*Colossians 3:17 (KJV)*

Today's Anchor: Maintain a high standard of executing the right way because it reflects who you are.

Unshakable Confidence

Preparation Is an Essential Part of Winning

Some people attack challenges confidently because they have done everything they can to prepare for battle. You can't win games, negotiations, business deals, and more without working hard before you engage.

Refining and customizing processes to a specific scenario sharpens all parts of your overall approach. When your opponent sees these elements are aligned, they will engage with more respect. If they look for weaknesses and find none, you have gained the upper hand before the battle is fought.

Preparation gives you confidence as you work toward the expected results you have invested in to provide you with a winner's edge.

"For which of you, intending to build a tower, sitteth not down."

—Luke 14:28 (KJV)

Today's Anchor: Winners prepare so pressure-filled situations are less likely to surprise them.

Building a Life That Lasts

The Value of Time

Why do we agree to trade time for money? Why do we negotiate what that time is worth differently than other commodities? Not knowing what your time is worth can cost you dearly.

Place your time at a premium and only do business with others who respect time as much as you do. This is how you work efficiently to optimize your opportunities and make the most of time and money.

Let your time and attention drive you to do bigger and better things. Raise the ceiling of your limiting beliefs and use your time wisely while increasing your financial capacity.

> *"So teach us to number our days, that we may apply our hearts unto wisdom."*
>
> *—Psalm 90:12 (KJV)*

Today's Anchor: Protect your time like it's money because it's more valuable.

Asking the Right Questions

When Was the Last Time You Took Stock?

How often do you take time out to genuinely reflect on where you're at in life? Have you considered what you need to do to optimize your life for the highest possible level of joy?

Doing so provides you with opportunity to express gratitude for all you've been given thus far, and to find ways to use those gifts to help others. How often do you think in these terms? What have you done in the past to repay the world for what you have received?

Life is challenging enough but when you take stock and change directions, you create momentum to push through those struggles.

"Let us search and try our ways, and turn again to the LORD."

—Lamentations 3:40 (KJV)

Today's Anchor: Taking a personal inventory creates clarity and enables you to adjust quickly.

What This Week Changed in Me

The Nature of Grace

Grace is one of those things that creates a hypocrite of us all. It's the one thing we want from everyone yet the one thing we are so reluctant to give.

To remove these feelings, remember the last time we needed or wanted it and what it felt like to not receive it. Reflecting on those insights, we might be more willing to hand out grace when it is requested.

Just as failure and falling short makes us human, so does our ability to forgive others and extend grace when a situation calls for it.

"And he said unto me, My grace is sufficient for thee."

—2 Corinthians 12:9 (KJV)

Today's Anchor: Grace doesn't lower the standard—it lifts you back into the fight.

Weekly Reflection:

____

____

____

____

____

____

Week 8

Staying the Course

Do Not Let Fear Guide You

It isn't easy, but you must fight through your fears when making decisions.

One of the best ways to fight through fear is to keep asking questions until you get all the answers you need to move forward with confidence. Knowledge replaces fear and is a powerful approach to success.

Be aware that you will increase your fear if you get information that is not truthful or biased. Deal in facts, not opinions, from those who have the expertise to share with you.

> *"Fear thou not; for I am with thee: be not dismayed; for I am thy God: I will strengthen thee; yea, I will help thee; yea, I will uphold thee with the right hand of my righteousness."*
>
> *—Isaiah 41:10 (KJV)*

Today's Anchor: Because fear is a liar, let faith call the plays today.

Strength Through the Struggle

Live Life with Perspective

Perspective is one of the most important tools we can employ to guide our thoughts.

It feeds the gratitude needed to push through adversity and embrace the blessings that we sometimes take for granted. It's the compass we need to remind us of where we're truly at in life, instead of letting short-term challenges overwhelm us. Using perspective also reminds of us our frailty as well as God's grace.

Let perspective guide and lead you when times are tough but also when you enjoy periods of prosperity, too.

> *"While we look not at the things which are seen, but at the things which are not seen: for the things which are seen are temporal; but the things which are not seen are eternal."*
>
> *—2 Corinthians 4:18 (KJV)*

Today's Anchor: Perspective shrinks problems and strengthens gratitude. Zoom out before you zoom in.

Winning the Ordinary Days

You Are Always Growing

You are never finished growing. As you finish growing in one area, you will transition to another. When this change happens, you can use your past successes to instill more confidence in challenges you're facing.

This is how we lift the veil on uncertainty and provide a blueprint for anything we set out to do. The key is to understand that this growth is not linear. There will be ups and downs, and failures and successes along the way.

> *"But grow in grace, and in the knowledge of our Lord and Saviour Jesus Christ. To him be glory both now and for ever. Amen."*
>
> *—2 Peter 3:18 (KJV)*

Today's Anchor: Stay committed to the process because growth is happening whether you feel it or not.

Unshakable Confidence

Visualizing the Finish Line

You can build confidence in any task by visualizing crossing the finish line early and often. This counters our natural tendencies of creating a negative bias that often plays in our heads and can be a big barrier to successfully completing any task.

This vision of an affirmative outcome over an affliction that stands in our way makes a difficult scenario into an achievable outcome. It makes a seemingly impossible task into a possible reality.

> *"Wherefore seeing we also are compassed about with so great a cloud of witnesses."*
>
> *—Hebrews 12:1 (KJV)*

Today's Anchor: Keep the finish line in your mind so you don't quit in the middle.

Building a Life That Lasts

The Importance of Gratitude

Be thankful for all that you are given, big and small. Appreciate all gifts and demonstrate your gratitude by paying it forward, sharing your gifts and good fortune with others.

The more gratitude you pour into your life, the more that will be given to you.

However, when much is given, much is also expected. You must create an expectation within you that the more you are given, the more you should share with the world. We are never meant to keep things to ourselves.

The best way to push forward with gratitude is by paying it forward with love and kindness in your heart.

"O give thanks unto the LORD, for he is good."

—Psalm 107:1 (KJV)

Today's Anchor: Gratitude turns what you have into enough while creating momentum.

Asking the Right Questions

What Expectations Do You Have?

Do you place higher expectations on others than on yourself? Are you able to accurately judge your talents and gifts so that your expectations align with reality? Can you do this as accurately with other people?

Expectations have a way of creating self-fulfilling outcomes. Do you find that when you have positive expectations of your actions, they turn out better than negative ones? You can frame those expectations either way.

Always include a gut check that ensures expectations for yourself and others are aligned with a positive outcome.

"For surely there is an end."

—Proverbs 23:18 (KJV)

Today's Anchor: Expectation without alignment creates frustration, so get clear on what you want.

What This Week Changed in Me

Taking Actions When Nobody Is Watching

What we do when others aren't looking is what defines the vision we want. When we quietly go about our business, and we do it with confidence, we create separation between who we are and who we want to be.

This is best done without unwanted outside influence and judgments about our plans. Simply executing what we want with the least amount of interference by those who don't understand what we want is the surest way to get what we are looking for.

"*That thine alms may be in secret.*"

—*Matthew 6:4 (KJV)*

Today's Anchor: Integrity is who you are in private.

Weekly Reflection:

____

____

____

____

____

____

Week 9

Staying the Course

Maintaining Self-Discipline

Self-discipline has many parts. We often assume it is determining an optimal routine for long periods to get the results we want. However, self-discipline is also about withholding things that don't serve you. You may want them, even if they don't align with your goals. It is up to you to set them aside for what you need.

We must also learn to sacrifice instant gratification for temperance and patience for what is unseen. This form of discipline requires a long-term approach, and you must understand that small intermediate sacrifices are worth it to reach the biggest goals ahead.

"But I keep under my body, and bring it into subjection."

—1 Corinthians 9:27 (KJV)

Today's Anchor: Self-discipline is self-respect. Do what you said you would do.

Strength Through the Struggle

Follow Negativity to Its Source

When you are stuck in a dark pool of negative thinking that does not serve you, follow those thoughts to their source.

Find that source, seek to understand it, and then fully embrace it so that you can redirect that energy to where you really want to go. Just like digging out weeds in a garden, you must remove negative thinking all the way down to its roots. This is the only way to clear a path for more productive and positive thinking. It frees you from using some of your energy worrying if that weed will grow back.

Just like weeding a garden, you must be diligent and keep redirecting those thoughts to a positive way of thinking.

Pulling those weeds of negativity is a choice, and when you take care in cultivating your garden, you will enjoy a bountiful harvest.

> *"O generation of vipers, how can ye, being evil, speak good things?"*
>
> *—Matthew 12:34 (KJV)*

Today's Anchor: Trace the negativity back to its root, then cut it off with truth.

Winning the Ordinary Days

Doing Extraordinary Things Without Applause

People like you do extraordinary things without notice. They are true to their cause and their capabilities. They don't need the approval of others. Doing the work and enjoying the outcomes are reward enough.

Do you know which God-given gifts allow you to do extraordinary things? Have you done an inventory of your skills and talents so you know where to concentrate your efforts?

It's up to you to draw on your inner strength to turn your thoughts into actions.

"For do I now persuade men, or God? or do I seek to please men? for if I yet pleased men, I should not be the servant of Christ."

—Galatians 1:10 (KJV)

Today's Anchor: Purpose doesn't need permission or praise.

Unshakable Confidence

Intentional Leadership

An important part of leadership is making sure you are intentional in helping others navigate through tough terrain. Good leaders enable those under them to forge their own paths, but they do so while also guiding them with guardrails of care.

Sometimes leaders must be vocal and firm. At other times, a good leader will provide growth opportunities to foster confidence in others much like the confidence they have in their own abilities. Do you have the confidence to let others step up and learn how to lead as well?

Confident leaders must be willing and patient to allow for this growth, understanding the value it provides for long-term job satisfaction and growth.

"A man's heart deviseth his way."

—Proverbs 16:9 (KJV)

Today's Anchor: Lead on purpose instead of drifting into decisions you'll have to clean up later.

Building a Life That Lasts

Time Is Our Most Valuable Asset

Time is our most precious and limited asset. Unlike money, once a moment of time is spent, it is gone forever. You can't accumulate more time. It is finite and, unfortunately, too often it is taken for granted.

Many people lose sight of the fact that they will not live forever and waste time foolishly, only to regret those lost moments later in life.

A smarter way to live is to savor as many moments as you can. Appreciate a special moment with someone you love, a conversation with an old friend, eating your favorite meal, or the joy of discovery that comes from reading a good book. Great moments don't need to cost you a penny but they are priceless in so many ways.

However you spend your time, always fill your heart with gratitude.

"Redeeming the time, because the days are evil."

—Ephesians 5:16 (KJV)

Today's Anchor: You can earn more money, but you can't earn more time so spend every moment with intention.

Asking the Right Questions

What Influences You?

Have you given much thought to what influences your thinking the most? Do you have full understanding of how they affect your life and assist you in deciding how you navigate your thoughts and actions? It's easy for flattery and ego to influence us but is it in the right direction for the right reasons?

When we remove ego and don't allow irrelevant forces into our decision-making it enables us to make decisions based on our original intentions.

The next time a potentially influential source boosts your ego, ask yourself if this influence is affecting you in a positive way, or if you are better off focusing on your own free will instead.

"Let us not therefore judge one another anymore."

—Romans 14:13 (KJV)

Today's Anchor: If it influences you, it shapes you, so choose what you allow in like your life depends on it.

What This Week Changed in Me

Tapping into Other People's Purpose

To fully inspire others to action, find their purpose and motivation. It's much more effective than trying to imprint our purpose and motivation on them and expect the best possible results. What they care about may be similar to ours on a high level, but deep down, they are working toward their own goals.

Great leaders know that effective teams are drawn to a common cause, and within that cause, each team member has individual goals and outcomes they want to see. Understanding this builds mutual trust to create alignment that moves the needle.

> *"Look not every man on his own things, but every man also to the interests of others."*
>
> *—Philippians 2:4 (KJV)*

Today's Anchor: The fastest way to grow is to help someone else grow.

Weekly Reflection:

____

____

____

____

____

____

Week 10

Staying the Course

Intention Creates Resilience

Focusing intensely on what matters most to you creates a raging resilience.

Small acts that feed into your goals create a suit of armor to fight off distractions and setbacks. You are more confident when you focus intensely on what you want. This enables you to bounce back quicker and get back on course to the destination you seek.

Reaffirm your intentions often. They are important reminders that can protect you from delays in the outcomes you want.

"Knowing this, that the trying of your faith worketh patience."

—James 1:3 (KJV)

Today's Anchor: Resilience is built by intentional choices you repeat.

Strength Through the Struggle

Overcoming the Fear of Self-Inspiration

Why does inspiration come so easily from others when we have so much within to pull from?

When we shy away from looking inward for inspiration, it's generally rooted in a fear from previous failures. What we fail to realize is that what has happened in the past is no guarantee it will happen in the future. People, situations, our personal growth, and more have changed. Knowing this, it can still be difficult to let go of what we believe about ourselves.

If you struggle this way, you can overcome these fears with God's grace. He knows your desires and what you are capable of, and would not place a desire in your heart unless He wanted you to be inspired to follow through in your pursuit of it.

Relying on His grace removes this mindset because through Him all things are possible.

> *"Wherefore I put thee in remembrance that thou stir up the gift of God, which is in thee by the putting on of my hands."*
>
> *—2 Timothy 1:6 (KJV)*

Today's Anchor: Stop waiting for a sign. You're the one God equipped to move first.

Winning the Ordinary Days

Creating a Unified Team

To become unstoppable as a leader, make sure your team's ideas and principles are clear, aligned, and unified. When you act, act as one. When you make changes, change as one.

The best way to build a unified mindset is through, clear, and consistent communication. Make sure messages are easy to understand and align with the greater purpose of the team. You must also build a team that fully buys into the principles and purpose at hand. This is how everyone wins in the short and long term.

> *"And if one prevail against him, two shall withstand him."*
>
> —*Ecclesiastes 4:12 (KJV)*

Today's Anchor: Unity is built with intention, not hope. Align the mission and watch momentum rise.

Unshakable Confidence

Fear Is the Enemy of Progress

When we feed into fear it can paralyze us. Nobody likes this feeling because we're built for faith, and leaning into fears is how we push through.

On the other side of fear, we often enjoy a feeling of fulfillment and accomplishment. Still, we hide from our fears and avoid direct contact, allowing fear to overcome us when we don't display courage.

Do whatever it takes internally and externally to look fear straight in the eye, with confidence, faith, and perseverance, to push through to the other side and win.

"What time I am afraid, I will trust in thee."

—Psalm 56:3 (KJV)

Today's Anchor: Progress starts when you act while you're still scared.

Building a Life That Lasts

Gratitude Is Wealth

Consistently practicing gratitude is the key to waking up with the unlimited fuel of contentment. It is difficult to put a price on contentment other than those who have it are the spiritually and emotionally the most wealthy among us.

You can find gratitude in all areas of your life. You must simply develop a mindset of abundance in things that are important and unimportant. That intentionality enables you to open your eyes to more possibilities in your life.

Gratitude is the fuel that fills your day with joy, peace, and love, making you wealthy in more ways than one.

"But godliness with contentment is great gain."

—1 Timothy 6:6 (KJV)

Today's Anchor: Be grateful because contentment is a form of wealth.

Asking the Right Questions

What Is Life Trying to Teach Us?

When we have a reaction to something, what is that event, and our reaction to it, trying to teach us? Are we able to ask pointed questions to help us understand why we reacted a certain way? Can we learn things about ourselves that we never knew?

Those of us who take life at face value without digging deeper miss much of the meaning that can propel our lives forward with greater understanding.

Can you be the person who wants to know the one you spend the most time with, which is you, by remaining curious as though you just met?

> *"For whatsoever things were written aforetime were written for our learning, that we through patience and comfort of the scriptures might have hope."*
>
> —*Romans 15:4 (KJV)*

Today's Anchor: Every season has a lesson born out of pain.

What This Week Changed in Me

In the Moment

Does your mind drift to other times, places, and people? How often do you let this get in the way of what's going on in your life right now?

When you are easily distracted by these things, you deny yourself the joy of being in the moment.

Instead of living in the past and creating regret or living in the future with anxiety, simply focus on the present to bring you the peace and gratitude you're looking for. That is how you find true enlightenment.

"Take therefore no thought for the morrow."

—Matthew 6:34 (KJV)

Today's Anchor: Be present. Today could be where your next win is built.

Weekly Reflection:

___

___

___

___

___

___

Week 11

Staying the Course

Digging In

When you're tired and don't see the results of your labor you must dig in even more. Intentional, focused work over a long period will produce results if you stay the course. Too many people give up too soon, and they never find the success or the person they were meant to be.

> *"Blessed is the man that endureth temptation."*
>
> —*James 1:12 (KJV)*

Today's Anchor: Choose to own the moment before the pressure decides how that moment will unfold.

Strength Through the Struggle

Respond to Failure

Failure happens to us whether we like it or not. However, when things don't go our way, we can choose how to respond. When we accept and learn from our failures, we grow. When we fight them, we become our worst enemy. Failures are one form of perseverance and an integral stepping stone to mastery.

When we achieve mastery, our perseverance is rewarded, and our discomfort zone doesn't paralyze us in self-pity.

"My flesh and my heart faileth."

—Psalm 73:26 (KJV)

Today's Anchor: Stay intentional. Control what you can, release what you can't, and keep moving toward your goal.

Winning the Ordinary Days

Align Actions and Motives

Stay consistent in aligning your actions with your motives. This alignment is only meaningful when those motives are pure in purpose and not selfish desires. Consistently generating this type of behavior overcomes our inner voice, which sometimes tells us what we want is not possible.

Repeatedly combining these two locks in our process until it becomes a habit. When you have created a habit, you will find it is much easier to move forward even at times when you struggle with limitations you place on yourself or the world puts in your way.

Let others fall into complacency that creates inconsistent actions. Those people choose reasons over results. You are not that type of person and you can prove it when you actively practice alignment in your actions and motives.

> *"But the LORD said unto Samuel, Look not on his countenance, or on the height of his stature; because I have refused him: for the LORD seeth not as man seeth; for man looketh on the outward appearance, but the LORD looketh on the heart."*
>
> *—1 Samuel 16:7 (KJV)*

Today's Anchor: Lock in your standards and don't deviate from them because your best future responds to what you do consistently.

Unshakable Confidence

Stay Calm

Keeping cool when provoked is a difficult but wise action for you and those on your team.

Staying calm in chaos is a sign of confidence. Meeting adversity with strength and clarity sets an example for others, including those who rely on us to lead them.

Unchecked emotions rarely carry us in the right direction. When you are confronted by a difficult challenge, take a step back, take a breath, weigh how you will respond and ask who will be affected by your response.

"Be still and know that I am God."

—Psalm 46:10 (KJV)

Today's Anchor: When adversity strikes, a pause is often required for a reset that will help you win.

Building a Life That Lasts

Confidence Produces Wealth

Deciding to build a dream is doable for everyone. Each of us can harness forward motion to create action in the direction we want to go, regardless of naysayers and the pointless expectations of others.

Dreams require courage and confidence to turn them into reality. As you pursue your dreams, learn to tap into the power of these gifts.

If you have doubts, ask yourself why you were selected to be the one to make a particular dream happen. It was planted in your heart by God, and if He thinks you are capable by giving you the gift of a dream, you are worthy of pursuing it by all means necessary.

> *"Honour the LORD with thy substance, and with the first fruits of all thine increase."*
>
> *—Proverbs 3:9–10 (KJV)*

Today's Anchor: Lock in to your dreams and return to them as quickly as possible when you get knocked off course.

Asking the Right Questions

Life Is Fragile

Why do we treat life as though it is made of steel, when in reality, life is fragile?

We often forget the value of our relationships with others and the simple pleasures we are gifted daily. Taking stock on these things by consistently practicing gratitude toward ourselves and others fills our cup while reconnecting us to the vine.

How often do you view life this way? What can you do to shift your mindset to appreciate more the fragile nature of life, the value of the relationships, and the pleasures you are given?

"Whereas ye know not what shall be on the morrow."

—James 4:14 (KJV)

Today's Anchor: Treat life for the delicate and precious gift that it is.

What This Week Changed in Me

Peace Is Wealth

Peace can be found in any situation if you look for it. Don't let strife make its home within you.

Ground yourself in what you know to be true not through the false seeds of doubt. These seeds will grow into weeds that can easily overtake you if you do not pull them quickly.

If you must, let your struggles only rent a small period of time in your life, then take back ownership by creating and acting upon solutions.

> *"And let the peace of God rule in your hearts, to the which also ye are called in one body; and be ye thankful."*
>
> *—Colossians 3:15 (KJV)*

Today's Anchor: Peace is a choice.

Weekly Reflection:

____

____

____

____

____

____

Week 12

Staying the Course

Magnets and Alignment

Are you attracting and using the tools that align with your vision?

For example, there are two sides of a magnet. Both sides perform important functions: either pulling you toward or pushing you away from your goals. If you use a magnet the wrong way, it will appear to not align with your goals. In reality, it is an important tool but you must know how to use it the right way.

Like many things, it's not the magnet's fault for doing what it naturally does if it's used the wrong way by the person making the decisions.

"Can two walk together, except they be agreed."

—*Amos 3:3 (KJV)*

Today's Anchor: What you tolerate, you invite. Keep your standards of others in alignment with your own.

Strength Through the Struggle

Quiet the Noise

Know where your fear comes from and shut it down by regrouping to the present moment and who you are now, combining it with gratitude and appreciation for the day and moment you are in.

> *"For I reckon that the sufferings of this present time are not worthy to be compared with the glory which shall be revealed in us."*
>
> *—Romans 8:18 (KJV)*

Today's Anchor: Turn the volume down and keep it simple because your next move needs clarity.

Winning the Ordinary Days

Narrowing Your Focus

Eliminating wasteful thoughts and actions is critical to pursuing the dreams you want to achieve. Shutting out distractions enables us to narrow our energy to daily habits. This creates opportunities much like dropping the first domino in a chain reaction of momentum toward the direction we have chosen.

When we scatter our energy and have diluted focus, we receive diluted results. Spend quality time thinking about what serves you well and what you can eliminate to help you intelligently commit to your goal.

"But one thing is needful."

—Luke 10:42 (KJV)

Today's Anchor: Depth beats width. Pick one lane and watch your confidence follow.

Unshakable Confidence

Quickly Return to Your Original Course

Quickly returning to your original course is a sign confident on your path forward. Temporary distractions can lead to bigger issues if you let them go unchallenged. How fast you pivot back on track will determine the amount of work that needs to be done to repair the damage.

The longer you stay off track the harder it is to return. Use today to recalibrate where you are, adjust as necessary, and move according to where you intend to go.

> *"Ponder the path of thy feet, and let all thy ways be established. Turn not to the right hand nor to the left: remove thy foot from evil."*
>
> —*Proverbs 4:26–27 (KJV)*

Today's Anchor: Distractions are inevitable and it's up to you to minimize them and get back on track as soon as possible.

Building a Life That Lasts

Discipline Is the Key to Success

Each of us defines success differently. However, the one thing all success has in common is that discipline is required to create financial, spiritual, emotional, and material wealth.

If you chase your version of success without the discipline you will fall into a pattern of a perpetual state of excuses.

There is only one excuse that matters. A lack of discipline. When you employ discipline and stack it with consistency, the successes you search for will miraculously follow suit.

> *"Exercise thyself rather unto godliness. For bodily exercise profiteth little: but godliness is profitable unto all things, having promise of the life that now is, and of that which is to come."*
>
> *—1 Timothy 4:7–8 (KJV)*

Today's Anchor: God honors the right reasons and the disciplined work you put in to make something become a reality.

Asking the Right Questions

Remove Dysfunctions

What dysfunctions have you been using to falsely fuel your passion?

We tend to hold onto things we know don't serve us because of their familiarity, even when it is toxic. You should ask yourself what dysfunctions you've been holding onto, because if you haven't figured it out yet, they are lies.

Understanding what they are is critical to detaching from them going forward. They are holding you back and removing them and the bad habits they create destroys false comforts you've sold yourself on as a necessity.

> *"That ye put off concerning the former conversation the old man, which is corrupt according to the deceitful lusts; And be renewed in the spirit of your mind."*
>
> *—Ephesians 4:22–23 (KJV)*

Today's Anchor: Removing dysfunctions increases the excellence in everything you do.

What This Week Changed in Me

Focus on This Moment

You can relive moments from your past anytime you want. Often, you'll dwell on the good and the bad. Doing too much of this robs you from the most important time of your life: the present.

Spend as much time as you can in the here and now. Be where your feet are. Actively listen and engage others with a grateful heart. Creating new moments with family, friends, and work associates helps you overcome adversity as you grow in new directions.

Future prosperity lives in the present moment. Focus on it and you will be rewarded in ways beyond what you can imagine.

> *"While it is said, Today if ye will hear his voice, do not harden your hearts as in the rebellion."*
>
> *—Hebrews 3:15 (KJV)*

Today's Anchor: Stand firm. Quitting isn't an option when your purpose is clear.

Weekly Reflection:

____

____

____

____

____

____

Week 13

Staying the Course

Don't Turn Pain into Blame

When you are hurt or angry, it's easy to get overwhelmed by negative emotions that can point blame at others. However, this isn't productive and makes things worse. It not only seeks to inflict your pain on others but also inflicts more pain on you.

As hard as it is, the best course of action is to either forgive, seek a measured response, or let go of the situation completely so you can move forward. Your time is limited so you must focus on positivity and productivity that doesn't weigh you down.

> *"Let all bitterness, and wrath, and anger . . . be put away from you . . ."*
>
> *—Ephesians 4:31–32 (KJV)*

Today's Anchor: Choose gratitude and forgiveness instead of anger and hurt.

Strength Through the Struggle

Reaching the Summit

So many people give up just before they reach the summit. They abandon perseverance even though the triggering obstacle is a much worse outcome than the effort required to meet their long-term goals.

Giving up before we start is one thing, but giving up just before we finish without knowing it is another. How many times have you done this in the past, finding out you were right there?! You experience feelings of regret and blame that linger when you don't stay the course and keep your blinders on until you reach your goal.

> *"But they that wait upon the LORD shall renew their strength."*
>
> *—Isaiah 40:31 (KJV)*

Today's Anchor: Perseverance is the key to reaching the summits in your life.

Winning the Ordinary Days

Stay Grounded and Humble

Some people let their egos take over when they experience a certain level of success. What they don't realize is that ego is an enemy that can blind and undermine future efforts.

Instead, it's better to stay grounded and humble in all situations. Do not deviate from who you are and your reasons for doing something. Simply learn to accept success and failure with the same mindset, getting neither too high or too low when either one happens.

> *"For I say, through the grace given unto me, to every man that is among you, not to think of himself more highly than he ought to think; but to think soberly."*
>
> *—Romans 12:3 (KJV)*

Today's Anchor: Don't let your insecurities drive you today. Stay confident and humble when you experience failure and success.

Unshakable Confidence

Learning New Skills Increases Confidence

Learning new skill sets that will fuel future desires is essential for growth.

Implementing them daily cements them into habits. As you become more comfortable with these habits, you will build confidence through repetition. The key is to educate yourself to the highest degree as you act on your desires.

This removes a lot of the doubts you may have, giving you the edge you need to compete with an edge against those who don't work as hard.

> *"Give instruction to a wise man, and he will be yet wiser: teach a just man, and he will increase in learning."*
>
> *—Proverbs 9:9 (KJV)*

Today's Anchor: When you grow, your confidence grows with you.

Building a Life That Lasts

Don't Take Gratitude for Granted

Gratitude comes in all sizes. It's easy to lean towards the obvious gifts in front of us but we must also practice of gratitude for the things we often take for granted.

These can be simple things like certain smells, beautiful sights, food, water, warmth, shelter, and more. Take the time to truly dive into the many areas of gratitude instead of waiting until you are without.

Many others are praying for what we have in front of us, so count your blessings, big and small.

> *"Enter into his gates with thanksgiving, and into his courts with praise."*
>
> *—Psalm 100:4 (KJV)*

Today's Anchor: What would you miss today if it was taken from you?

Asking the Right Questions

Do You Have Limiting Beliefs?

Chances are you think about some things in certain ways that keep you from moving forward without hesitation. That's normal but take that awareness and ask yourself why.

What stands in your way? What holds you back? Is it old beliefs from your past? What happened that caused you to think this way?

When we were young, we didn't have these limitations. There were no caps on our thoughts, dreams, and imagination. But as we grow older, we build walls around ourselves until we are unable to see the light that once shone through.

What parts of this wall do you need to remove to let the light of dreams and possibilities shine through again?

Is it time to tear down those walls and begin living a life free from limits that no longer serve you well. The answer is yes. It is time to start building bridges to your future, instead of staying behind the walls of your past.

"Be careful for nothing."

—Philippians 4:6 (KJV)

Today's Anchor: Eliminate your limiting beliefs by repeating those things that propel you forward.

What This Week Changed in Me

Peeling Off the Mask

Will you allow yourself to be vulnerable enough to remove the masks that you often hide behind? There are scripts we follow based on things we learned in life that are no longer true.

The masks that once served us well are now masks of betrayal and removing them will enable you to live more genuine going forward. Your genuine self, not the shadow of who you once were, is where the greatness lies and is what is meant to be shared with the world.

"The fear of the LORD is the beginning of wisdom."

—Proverbs 9:10 (KJV)

Today's Anchor: Today, live in the moment of who you are and not what others expect you to be.

Weekly Reflection:

____

____

____

____

____

____

Week 14

Staying the Course

Taking an Important Pause

Pausing to assess a situation provides perspective that can only be attained by weighing options before acting. It is a powerful tool you can use in your favor if you remain disciplined in your approach.

A pause lets you gauge potential outcomes more accurately, ask questions to gather more information, and calm any emotions that may interfere with your decision-making process. This leads to results that move your purpose forward.

However extreme or obvious a circumstance might seem, taking the time to put it in perspective enables you to enjoy the outcomes without regret.

> *"Come unto me, all ye that labour and are heavy laden, and I will give you rest."*
>
> *—Matthew 11:28 (KJV)*

Today's Anchor: "Ask, listen, then move" is how you build momentum.

Strength Through the Struggle

Infinite Growth

Infinite growth is a positive mindset that enables you to reframe a negative driver that threatens to knock you off course. Reframing negatives by turning them into learning experiences or looking for positives in a poor outcome can lead you to new paths that keep you in an infinite growth mindset.

This drives the darkness out of your life as you light paths of positivity. If you're lost after a setback, revisit your purpose and you'll rediscover an infinite growth mindset that will point you in the right direction.

"Thy word is a lamp unto my feet, and a light unto my path."

—Psalm 119:105 (KJV)

Today's Anchor: Stay rooted and don't be swayed by temporary storms in your life.

Winning the Ordinary Days

Intentions Combined with Actions Create Joy

When you set your mind on something you want to accomplish and then act on those intentions, you will produce joy in your life. That joy comes from a sense of accomplishment and a feeling that anything is possible.

Intentions that are never acted on feed complacency. Actions without clear thoughts create confusion that ultimately produce poor results. This is the form of misery that leads to stagnation.

Keep dreaming and keep moving toward those dreams. Remember, taking no action produces no joy.

"In all labour there is profit."

—*Proverbs 14:23 (KJV)*

Today's Anchor: Act early, and your future you will thank you.

Unshakable Confidence

Getting Out of Your Comfort Zone

One of the best things you can do is to get out of your comfort zone. When you do this, you watch the nature of your true self reveal over time.

Getting out of your comfort zone requires discipline and focus because your brain, by default, likes living in comfort. It always seeks the known as a way to protect you. You can't let this mindset get in your way.

Despite these things, you must stay steadfast and true to your goal of who you want to be. Veer away from comfort and lean into the insecurity.

Discipline, minus comfort, plus consistency, equals evolution.

> *"For my thoughts are not your thoughts, neither are your ways my ways, saith the LORD. For as the heavens are higher than the earth, so are my ways higher than your ways, and my thoughts than your thoughts."*
>
> —*Isaiah 55:8–9 (KJV)*

Today's Anchor: Leaning into your uncomfortable zone is where the most growth in you will take place.

Building a Life That Lasts

Properly Living in the Moment

Life moves forward. While we have some say in the direction, forces beyond our control can make us change course whether we like it or not.

Despite these unforeseen shifts, it's important for us to show up, react with restraint, and stay focused on where we want to go. When our conviction is strong, the only thing that changes is how we're going to get there.

You can dwell on the past and dream about the future, but unless you focus on the present, and frame it the right way, your path will always be in doubt. Don't let this happen!

"And also that every man should eat and drink, and enjoy the good of all his labour, it is the gift of God."

—Ecclesiastes 3:13 (KJV)

Today's Anchor: Lead with faith to guide you in the right direction.

Asking the Right Questions

Do You Have Everything You Need?

You can look at life two ways. Do you have everything you need? Or do you need everything you have?

Which of these statements ring truer for you?

When you're honest with yourself, you will find these answers in how you see things in your world.

> *"For what shall it profit a man, if he shall gain the whole world, and lose his own soul?"*
>
> *—Mark 8:36 (KJV)*

Today's Anchor: You are enough; striving is just for fun.

What This Week Changed in Me

Drifting or Directed?

Are you drifting or directed?

When you have the right habits, they will drive you to pursue a relentless path of learning. At times, this will happen because you failed. But if you are smart enough to learn the lesson behind those failures, and keep working hard, you will reach the top.

Make sure you are properly aligned for growth and not paralyzed by the fear of failure. Use that failure to keep you moving forward.

> *"I will instruct thee and teach thee in the way which thou shalt go."*
>
> —*Psalm 32:8 (KJV)*

Today's Anchor: Decide quickly because commitment ends debate.

Weekly Reflection:

____

____

____

____

____

____

Week 15

Staying the Course

Remain Grounded in Your Core Values

Remain grounded in your beliefs and core values when deciding your path. As you discover new information and people who want to sway you to what they believe, it's critical to not lose sight of what you are about.

Surround yourself with those who align with what you want to accomplish. This will strengthen and speed up your efforts, fortifying you against being pulled off course.

Who you were in the past is less important than who you are now. Incorporate the lessons and wisdom you have learned but remember that God provides us with a clear way forward if we choose to take it.

> *"Rooted and built up in him, and stablished in the faith, as ye have been taught, abounding therein with thanksgiving."*
>
> —*Colossians 2:7 (KJV)*

Today's Anchor: Remaining grounded in who you are makes it easier to get up every time you get knocked down. Falling isn't failure, but staying down is.

Strength Through the Struggle

Proactive Preparation Is the Key

Hoping for the best but preparing for the worst is simple but not easy. With so many competing demands for your time, knowing what needs to be done and acting on it are two different things. This allocation of your limited time and resources is a constant balancing act.

Learn to look to the future and spend time analyzing scenarios from different perspectives to give you the best decision on how to proceed. These types of decisions are not easy and may not be popular but if you want to be an effective leader, you must become an expert at diagnosing a situation as early as possible.

"The thoughts of the diligent tend only to plenteousness."

—Proverbs 21:5 (KJV)

Today's Anchor: Pause and prepare for the priorities that matter most.

Winning the Ordinary Days

Tuning Out Unnecessary Noise

One of the worst kinds of noise is comparison. When you compare yourself to others it robs you of your greatness and provides no value because your potential is limitless and still unfolding.

Each of our unique gifts come together much like musical instruments in an orchestra. We all play together but it is foolish to compare a trumpet to a drum.

> *"Brethren, I count not myself to have apprehended: but this one thing I do, forgetting those things which are behind, and reaching forth unto those things which are before, I press toward the mark."*
>
> *—Philippians 3:13–14 (KJV)*

Today's Anchor: Stop comparing yourself to others. You are on a unique journey that is yours alone.

Unshakable Confidence

Choose Faith over Fear

Faith over fear is the bridge we need to cross in times of doubt. It can carry us anywhere we want to go. Faith is the unseen belief you are worthy and have the ability to do what seems to be impossible. It can be intimidating for some people but when we lean into faith and push fear aside, we become powerful.

Make faith your superpower and use it to grow into what you're fully capable of. Do this, and you'll quickly realize that fear is the enemy of peace. When this happens, do everything in your power to leave it behind as far as you can.

"Be strong and of a good courage, fear not, nor be afraid . . ."

—Deuteronomy 31:6 (KJV)

Today's Anchor: Choose courage over chaos, and faith over fear.

Building a Life That Lasts

Joy Is a Form of Wealth

When you find joy in the work you do, you will rise above the unenjoyable parts of your day and minimize their impact. You can't force joy where there is none, but you can rewire your brain to seek it out, which it will do if you tell it to.

The added benefit is that joyful people are generally more successful in their life. They deal with less stress, burnout, frustration, and a lack of gratitude. It is the key that unlocks financial, spiritual, and emotional wealth. Seek it out and celebrate it every chance you get.

> *"Go your way, eat the fat, and drink the sweet, and send portions unto them for whom nothing is prepared: for this day is holy unto our Lord: neither be ye sorry; for the joy of the LORD is your strength."*
>
> *—Nehemiah 8:10 (KJV)*

Today's Anchor: Seek moments of joy in all that you do today.

Asking the Right Questions

Do You Think Big Thoughts?

What is your idea of big thinking? Do those thoughts excite you or scare you? Are you ready to step up and take on challenges that seem unattainable?

Most people play it safe and live with thoughts that are smaller or limiting more than they should be. Does this sound like you? If so, what are you afraid of?

Stretching your thinking to expand beyond what you thought possible is the only way for you to achieve them.

Are you ready to accept the challenge of big thinking and then taking the steps to put your thoughts into action?

> *"Now unto him that is able to do exceeding abundantly above all that we ask or think, according to the power that worketh in us."*
>
> *—Ephesians 3:20 (KJV)*

Today's Anchor: What would you do if you could? Because you can.

What This Week Changed in Me

Decide on Your Level of Commitment

When you enter into a new job, a project, or anything requiring an amount of your valuable time, you must decide how committed you are to seeing it through. Are you 100% in or are you only partially interested?

If you can't fully commit, it will undermine your ability to think you can get the outcome you desire.

Mindset is everything. Decide early on that you are committed, not just interested, and you will win more often.

"But Daniel purposed in his heart that he would not defile himself . . ."

—Daniel 1:8 (KJV)

Today's Anchor: Today, practice with your actions, not just your words.

Weekly Reflection:

____

____

____

____

____

____

Week 16

Staying the Course

Get Back Up After You Fall

You will get knocked down in life. When this happens, you must decide if you will get back up and how you will do it. The best place to start is by listening to the direction God has called for you. He knows your heart best and will guide you to the best way to recover from your setbacks.

How quickly you get back up depends on you. To minimize setbacks, it's best to not dwell on your failures. Instead, get up quickly, assess where you're at and where God wants you to be and move in that direction.

Do this no matter how many times you fall. Stay focused on your humility and use purpose as your flashlight.

> *"For a just man falleth seven times, and riseth up again."*
>
> *—Proverbs 24:16 (KJV)*

Today's Anchor: Courage is about overcoming fear to do challenging things in your life.

Strength Through the Struggle

Avoiding Emotional Derailment

What distracts you from your goals? In a world of endless distractions, how often do you find yourself emotionally derailed by things outside your control?

This can lead to the mistake of falling into a rabbit hole of skepticism instead of basic execution. Skepticism creates barriers while execution moves the needle to solve many of our concerns.

Avoid things that derail you and start executing what keeps you on track and headed in the right direction.

"Wait on the LORD."

—Psalm 27:14 (KJV)

Today's Anchor: Avoid negative emotions that can easily knock you off course.

Winning the Ordinary Days

Push Through It and Keep Going

When you accomplish something hard, there is always something equally challenging or more difficult ahead. Each task you complete means you have leveled up to bigger things. To succeed at this higher level, you must remain consistent in your approach.

Use your past successes as a daily reminder that you are capable of doing what is required to win. You already have the formula for success inside of you but it's up to you to put it to work.

"The righteous also shall hold on his way . . ."

—Job 17:9 (KJV)

Today's Anchor: Receive the gift of knowing that God wired you on purpose, for a purpose.

Unshakable Confidence

Self-Discipline and Momentum

Self-discipline is doing the work required to achieve mastery for things we do and don't want to do. To make this approach easier, it's critical to remember that small steps of discipline over time become big leaps in momentum.

To be as efficient as possible, keep momentum pointed toward the end result you're searching for. A loss of momentum will find its roots in the loss of self-discipline. You may get to where you're going, but you'll spend a lot more energy and time to accomplish your goal.

> *"And every man that striveth for the mastery is temperate in all things. Now they do it to obtain a corruptible crown; but we an incorruptible."*
>
> *—1 Corinthians 9:25 (KJV)*

Today's Anchor: Discipline and momentum create growth that creates proof you're alive.

Building a Life That Lasts

Draw from the Experience of Others

At times, you will have innovative and breakthrough moments that will lead you down a path less chosen based on your confidence and desire for self-reliance. There is nothing wrong with this path, but it isn't your only option or always the best.

Don't get stuck in the stubborn ways as you attempt to grow and be fully independent. Blend that mindset with the counsel of others so that you can stay on course and move forward faster than you can on your own.

> *"Iron sharpeneth iron; so a man sharpeneth the countenance of his friend."*
>
> *—Proverbs 27:17 (KJV)*

Today's Anchor: Seek counsel in the areas you are most stuck.

Asking the Right Questions

How Often Do You Dwell on the Past?

Do you spend time beating yourself up over past actions? Do you let these negative thoughts invade where you are now? The only time past thoughts are relevant is when you're able to frame them positively to encourage the next steps in your life. Understand that even when your past has not been kind you can still learn and grow from it.

We must constantly isolate negative thoughts and replace them with encouraging visions to protect our minds, using previous failures as learning experiences to benefit us now.

> *"This is the day which the LORD hath made; we will rejoice and be glad in it."*
>
> —*Psalm 118:24 (KJV)*

Today's Anchor: Keep evolving. Don't dwell on the past or freeze in an old version of who you were.

What This Week Changed in Me

Humility and Gratitude

Make sure people are seen and heard through the filter of humility. This sets the tone for a positive and productive exchange as you seek to understand what others truly need from you.

Humility is closely linked to gratitude, which you must also practice every chance you get. When you and the people you interact with practice these things, you can quickly reach an understanding with common ground.

Be generous with humility and gratitude, and in return they will fill your life with abundance.

> *"For who maketh thee to differ from another."*
>
> *—1 Corinthians 4:7 (KJV)*

Today's Anchor: Give it away knowing that what you share multiplies.

Weekly Reflection:

____

____

____

____

____

____

Week 17

Staying the Course

Leaning In During Challenging Times

When the odds are stacked against us and the outcome we want seems impossible, that's when we must dig deeper and lean in the most. It's easier when we're motivated, but it is even more necessary when we are not.

In those times when everything seems to be going in the opposite direction, that's when you need to put your head down and charge harder in the direction that leads you to success.

Dreams always have headwinds, which is why they aren't called guarantees.

"Now the God of hope fill you with all joy and peace . . ."

—Romans 15:13 (KJV)

Today's Anchor: Remember, action breaks mental and emotional paralysis.

Strength Through the Struggle

Avoid Comparisons

Unless there is a specific purpose attached, do not allow comparisons to take hold in your mind. No two situations or people are alike, and when you create comparisons, you create one that is sure to fall short.

Instead, move forward with faith in your own way and direction. Don't get distracted by what others are doing. That is their journey, not yours. Control what you can and don't worry about others. You have enough other things on your plate to worry about that you can't control.

> *"But let every man prove his own work, and then shall he have rejoicing in himself alone, and not in another."*
>
> *—Galatians 6:4 (KJV)*

Today's Anchor: Control what you can, release what you can't, and keep moving.

Winning the Ordinary Days

Discipline Defined

Discipline is the mastery of doing what one doesn't want to do. Small steps of discipline over time become big leaps in momentum.

Discipline can be flexible within a given framework, but you must not deviate or lose sight of the big picture. It is all about maintaining energy and flow, building habits so that your level of discipline becomes second nature and serves you well, instead of viewing discipline as another barrier to overcome.

> *"Therefore I say unto you, Take no thought for your life, what ye shall eat, or what ye shall drink; nor yet for your body, what ye shall put on."*
>
> *—Matthew 6:25 (KJV)*

Today's Anchor: You don't have to want to do it; you just have to do it.

Unshakable Confidence

The Roots of Analysis Paralysis

Analysis paralysis is all about making excuses and allowing ourselves to get stuck in between where we are and where we want to be.

If you lack confidence, you will want to dig to find answers that don't influence what you're working to accomplish. You're trying to find confirmation about which way to go when you should be focusing on *go* as the most effective way to move forward.

When you know where you want to go, you must dive in and see what happens. Confidence comes from trusting yourself and accepting that implementation and execution, and not perfection, are what matters most.

"I have set the LORD always before me."

—Psalm 16:8 (KJV)

Today's Anchor: One foot in front of the other in the direction you choose is the plan.

Building a Life That Lasts

Taking Time to Be Thankful

Taking time to be thankful for what you have been given will protect you from the dangers of self-pity, anger, sadness, and comparisons.

It's so common for the path of "not good enough" to grab hold in a world that is always looking for more. The reality is we already have so much more than we need or deserve.

Remember, nothing is a given but all has been given by God to use for His purpose. We should share these gifts, with joy, never looking back to what could or should have been.

If they were supposed to be a part of our life, they would.

> *"It is vain for you to rise up early, to sit up late, to eat the bread of sorrows: for so he giveth his beloved sleep."*
>
> *—Psalm 127:2 (KJV)*

Today's Anchor: Let go of worrying about what you don't have because you already have all that you need.

Asking the Right Questions

Why Do We Wait So Long?

Do you know why you procrastinate on some things? Why do we wait until our bodies and minds are at their weakest before we decide what to do? What are the fears and misconceptions we have about ourselves that keep us from moving forward now?

If you're stuck, these are important questions to ask. When you ask them often, your mind and body will be more in sync for you to move forward. Be proactive in adjusting before you're forced to do so in less favorable conditions. Working through these questions and not being afraid of the answers saves valuable time and energy to conquer your goals.

"Boast not thyself of tomorrow."

—Proverbs 27:1 (KJV)

Today's Anchor: Refuse to accept fear as a reason for procrastination.

What This Week Changed in Me

Learning from the Past

Previous generations have left us with a road map of what and what not to do. Past successes and mistakes are extremely beneficial to teach us what to focus on and what to avoid as we make our way in the world.

Sometimes, when we don't pay attention to the lessons of the past, we allow arrogance and ignorance to overtake common sense. This lack of reflection is a recipe for failure.

Today, take time to reflect on the lessons that others have provided to you. What have you learned, good and bad, that can positively influence where you're at today?

> *"Remember the days of old, consider the years of many generations: ask thy father, and he will shew thee; thy elders, and they will tell thee."*
>
> *—Deuteronomy 32:7 (KJV)*

Today's Anchor: Stay grateful by reflecting on your past achievements, knowing that joy grows where thankfulness lives.

Weekly Reflection:

____

____

____

____

____

____

Week 18

Staying the Course

What's Holding You Back?

The more you think about what's holding you back, the easier it is to focus on it and take steps to leave it behind. Give yourself permission to move forward without it, and you'll feel lighter than ever before.

Sometimes you need to say goodbye to people, jobs, relationships, or bad financial deals to make room for others that better serve you. This is tough because we tend to hold onto things that are meant to provide temporary education as if they are permanent teachers.

Look for new opportunities to push you to greater heights instead of staying stuck in those that weigh you down. Be transparent with yourself to find the clear path you should follow.

"He becometh poor that dealeth with a slack hand."

—Proverbs 10:4 (KJV)

Today's Anchor: Answer the question of what's holding you back and build momentum to propel you forward.

Strength Through the Struggle

Seek Higher Degrees of Difficulty

When we accomplish something hard, there is always something more challenging that lines up behind it. This may discourage some people, but the truth is that more challenging situations are a gift we receive that helps us grow to our full potential.

Let your past successes be your daily reminder that you need to keep going. You have everything you need to get to the next level. Don't shy away from those tasks; embrace them for the gifts they are.

> *"For our light affliction, which is but for a moment, worketh for us a far more exceeding and eternal weight of glory."*
>
> *—2 Corinthians 4:17 (KJV)*

Today's Anchor: Seek more challenging situations to create maximum growth in you.

Winning the Ordinary Days

Consistency and Purity

Stay consistent in aligning your actions and motives. Make sure those motives are pure in purpose, not selfish desires. When consistent actions and pure motives are aligned and repeated, we can accomplish what our inner voice won't always say is possible.

Follow the process, make it a habit, and keep doing it even when you don't want to. Let others fall back into complacent reasons over results, not you.

> *"Prepare thy work without, and make it fit for thyself in the field."*
>
> —*Proverbs 24:27 (KJV)*

Today's Anchor: Keep it clean. Integrity is always worth it.

Unshakable Confidence

Facing Fear in the Eyes

Having faith means you can do anything you put your mind to. It means facing fear in the eyes until it blinks. The fear of what will happen if you fail or succeed is the only thing stopping you from unleashing your intentions.

Once you get over this fear, there is nothing that can stand in your way. You can move forward with confidence and clear conscience to the things you want the most.

"Watch ye, stand fast in the faith, quit you like men, be strong."

—1 Corinthians 16:13 (KJV)

Today's Anchor: Own your choices by implementing your standard at all times.

Building a Life That Lasts

We Are Judged by What We Complete

Completion is everything. Too many times, we don't finish what we've started out of fear of failure.

The reality is when we don't finish, we create a self-fulfilling opinion of who we are by adding to our fears of not being good enough, not having enough talent, resources, or desire to get the job done. This is why you need to be your greatest cheerleader to create a champion who knows how to finish and enjoy victories.

Accept big challenges. Play the game in a big way, finish strong, and complete your tasks. In this way, regardless of the results, you win.

> *"Being confident of this very thing, that he which hath begun a good work in you will perform it until the day of Jesus Christ."*
>
> *—Philippians 1:6 (KJV)*

Today's Anchor: Be patient and stay the course until you complete the important tasks in front of you.

Asking the Right Questions

Extraordinary Gifts

What extraordinary gifts do you possess that make your life and the lives of others better? Have you worked to develop this gift to the highest degree possible?

You must know where your strengths and talents are so that you can use them with intention to move the needle. You may not fully understand what those talents are yet. It requires examining what's in your heart and how to draw it out.

Have you asked yourself and others what they think your biggest gifts are? What do you naturally gravitate to? Do you find it easier to do than other people?

Trust your gut and when it tells you the way forward; listen closely. That is how you make the biggest impact.

"I will praise thee."

—Psalm 139:14 (KJV)

Today's Anchor: Stay in your zone of genius and joy as long as possible.

What This Week Changed in Me

Changing Perspective Is Healthy

Changing your perspective can happen in a single moment or over time. Perspective is healthy because it means you're open and flexible when new things appear in your life.

How and when it happens is less important than the fact that you are open to shifting how you view things. Sometimes these decisions are easy because they are obvious. Other times, you will need to carefully weigh options, allowing new ideas time to take root.

If you don't understand, ask questions. Investigate as much as you need to feel comfortable with changing your mind or staying consistent with the perspective you have now.

> *"For to be carnally minded is death; but to be spiritually minded is life and peace."*
>
> *—Romans 8:6 (KJV)*

Today's Anchor: Where can you find perspective in adversity?

Weekly Reflection:

____

____

____

____

____

____

Week 19

Staying the Course

Remain Calm

You are faced with several decisions daily and it's up to you to decide how to confront them. It makes no sense to become emotional and lose objectivity. Instead, stay calm in the eye of a storm. Don't allow emotions to take control and lead you to poor choices.

If a situation doesn't go your way, remind yourself it doesn't mean it isn't going the right way. We must remember it's in times of adversity and frustration when the unseen blessings reside on the other side.

Find the lesson in your strife and use it to prepare for other battles in the future. The best way to do this is to think objectively and do your best to move on so the same battles don't resurface again.

> *"Pride goeth before destruction, and an haughty spirit before a fall."*
>
> *—Proverbs 16:18 (KJV)*

Today's Anchor: Remember to respond and not react to situations outside your control.

Strength Through the Struggle

Are You Afraid of Change?

Change is necessary for growth but it can be hard when it doesn't yield immediate results.

However, in your heart, if you know that change is good, especially when your current efforts keep yielding the same results that don't serve your goals, then change course!

When you know what you need to do but don't take action, you become paralyzed, and even though you might want to blame others, the fact remains that your lack of actions falls squarely on you.

"Therefore if any man be in Christ, he is a new creature . . ."

—2 Corinthians 5:17 (KJV)

Today's Anchor: What change is mandatory today?

Winning the Ordinary Days

Practice Consistency over Time

Planting seeds and expecting fruit to appear instantly is not reasonable, but today, it is expected in many areas of our lives. The speed at which life moves in some ways, from microwaves and online retailers to banking and more, moves at a dizzying rate.

Many people are impatient, and when they don't see immediate, big-picture results, they give up and move on, often to things that don't move the needle in their lives. For them, perseverance is still a ghost, a lesson yet to be learned, not understanding that those who persevere end up with a larger harvest than they ever imagined.

> *"For ye have need of patience, that, after ye have done the will of God, ye might receive the promise."*
>
> *—Hebrews 10:36 (KJV)*

Today's Anchor: Your future responds to what you do consistently.

Unshakable Confidence

You Are Constantly Evolving

The changes taking place in you are constant. Do not believe in who you once were. Instead believe in the evolution of who you are now. This makes it easier to care little about what others think. They can't fully understand how you're changing and what the true present version of you is.

These changes don't need to be dramatic. Small changes that constantly take place set in motion the ability to achieve small, consistent, and better versions of who you are to be. Changes of who you were yesterday by 1% are enough. Stack these days to get to your untapped potential of greatness.

> *"But the path of the just is as the shining light, that shineth more and more unto the perfect day."*
>
> *—Proverbs 4:18 (KJV)*

Today's Anchor: Stay teachable, knowing that correction is protection.

Building a Life That Lasts

The Gift of Sharing

Sharing experiences and gifts with others should be high on your list of purpose. Others can learn and benefit from the challenges you've been through. They can be inspired by how you've overcome those challenges if you're vulnerable and genuine. There are many ways to set an example while offering wisdom.

Remain disciplined and be a model of courage for others to follow. This is how you shine a light for others to emulate.

> *"But the manifestation of the Spirit is given to every man to profit withal."*
>
> *—1 Corinthians 12:7 (KJV)*

Today's Anchor: Sharing your abundance with others is one of the most fundamental character traits you can possess.

Asking the Right Questions

Are You Taking Immediate Action?

It is easy to critique ourselves on what we should have been done after the fact. We do it often when we don't get what we want.

If that's the case, then why is it we don't take immediate action to correct different situations? What is it inside of us that keeps us from acting with immediate attention and intention? Are we afraid of failure? Do we care enough about the outcome? What is it that motivated us to get involved in the first place?

When we can find answers to these questions, we'll stop thinking about "should haves" and "what-ifs" and, instead, pursue actions to get better outcomes.

> *"Therefore to him that knoweth to do good, and doeth it not, to him it is sin."*
>
> —*James 4:17 (KJV)*

Today's Anchor: Make the call, bold moves open doors.

What This Week Changed in Me

Collaboration Versus Dependency

Collaboration means every member of a team brings value to a task or a longer-term goal. Instead of depending on others to do things for us, when we reciprocate and add our skills to the mix, we are investing in a shared vision requiring focused effort on our part. This investment has a compounding effect that means while we are stacking wins, so is everyone else whom we collaborate with.

That is much different than sitting back and watch others do the work. Dependency invites poorer outcomes that can cost time, money, and missed opportunities.

"Two are better than one."

—Ecclesiastes 4:9 (KJV)

Today's Anchor: Joining with others for a specific outcome produces outsized results.

Weekly Reflection:

____

____

____

____

____

____

Week 20

Staying the Course

Pulling Weeds of Destruction

Don't let seeds of doubt take root in your mind. These small seeds can grow into weeds of destruction that hold back your potential for greatness. They must be removed as soon as you discover them or they will spread and inhibit the growth you are looking for.

They can be planted by others or inadvertently by you. Until we figure out their true nature, and remove them, we also make the mistake of watering them and allow them to take hold. This is why we must be vigilant and remove them as quickly as possible.

It's time to ask yourself what seeds have been planted in your mind that you must tend to and remove today.

"But ye, brethren, be not weary in well doing."

—2 Thessalonians 3:13 (KJV)

Today's Anchor: Removing negative seeds of doubt must be a priority in your life.

Strength Through the Struggle

Don't Let Your Frustrations Overtake You

Don't allow your frustrations to get the best of you. These feelings are temporary and the more you let them dominate your life, the more they will dig in, take root, and run deeper.

Rewire your brain to let a solution, action-based mindset take root instead. Action builds hope and confidence, which can turn a seemingly hopeless situation into a winning one. When you act, the impossible becomes possible. People will rally to your cause.

"When thou passest through the waters, I will be with thee."

—Isaiah 43:2 (KJV)

Today's Anchor: Stay thankful armed with the knowledge that complaining blinds you.

Winning the Ordinary Days

Protecting Your Mind

Protecting your mind and what you feed it is as important as anything you do each day. Be careful about what you decide to absorb every day because what you choose to let in defines you on the inside and what the world sees from you on the outside.

If you don't like the current version of you, change your environment, what you consume, and the people you associate with. These things, more than any others, have the most significant influence on your reaching your full potential.

> *"And the peace of God, which passeth all understanding, shall keep your hearts and minds through Christ Jesus."*
>
> *—Philippians 4:7 (KJV)*

Today's Anchor: Reset fast and don't stay stuck in a bad moment any longer than necessary.

Unshakable Confidence

Do Not Be a Victim

When you tell yourself you're a victim, you give yourself permission to accept failure.

Instead, accept what is happening and use it as motivation to fuel growth instead of groveling in blame that leads you on a path to nowhere.

How you choose to use your failures, either as lessons or excuses, determines the kind of life you will lead. The more we learn from failures, the faster we resolve shortcomings so we can move forward.

> *"Nay, in all these things we are more than conquerors through him that loved us."*
>
> —*Romans 8:37 (KJV)*

Today's Anchor: Be the victor of your mind, not the victim.

Building a Life That Lasts

Living Your Best Life Requires Periods of Restoration

You are not a super human. You are human, and as such, you must include periods of mind and body restoration to go to the next level. You simply can't keep going without a break.

Restoration is not complacency. It is a period of silence that is critical to refocus our efforts, practice gratitude, and get fired up for what comes next.

"He restoreth my soul."

—Psalm 23:3 (KJV)

Today's Anchor: Restoring your mind and body is refueling for the future.

Asking the Right Questions

Are You Holding On to the Wrong Things?

Do you hold on to dysfunctions because they are familiar? Do you fear growth and change causing you to accept less than you deserve? Are you ready to find new levels of passion to fuel your life and propel you to greater rewards?

Holding on to past ways of doing things and relationships that no longer serve you well is common. If this is you, have you thought about what it will take to detach from what's holding you back? Have you also thought about why you're holding on when common sense dictates you should be doing something else?

Removing bad habits and people who have produced small and fake rewards is essential if you want true success at a deeper and more satisfying level.

"And ye shall know the truth, and the truth shall make you free."

—John 8:32 (KJV)

Today's Anchor: Free yourself from holding onto things that no longer serve you.

What This Week Changed in Me

Change by Choice

The changes you make inside of you are yours to make. You are constantly evaluating and deciding if, how, and when to change. These changes can be overwhelming unless you also remember your goals and motivations.

The world already forces changes on you that you can't always control. This is why it's critical to be mindful of those things that you can. Using your values and standards will steer you on the right course, but you must also apply changing conditions and intentional focus to ensure the new path you've chosen is the right one.

"And be renewed in the spirit of your mind."

—Ephesians 4:23 (KJV)

Today's Anchor: Choose joy; strength follows gladness.

Weekly Reflection:

____

____

____

____

____

____

Week 21

Staying the Course

Focus on the Present Moment

Not all things in the mind are real; however, with enough intentional focus they can be made real.

That is why it's so important to pay attention to where your focus is aimed. Focusing on the past or the future creates useless anxiety. A better way to approach life is by focusing on the present moment when you can actually do something.

Spending too much time worrying about what was or what might be only heightens unnecessary feelings of perseverance when we can act in the present moment instead.

"*. . . exhort one another daily, while it is called today . . .*"

—*Hebrews 3:13 (KJV)*

Today's Anchor: Past noise is a test that threatens the more important focus of the here and now.

Strength Through the Struggle

The Overlooked Benefits of Adversity

Few people enjoy adversity. It's uncomfortable and creates stress and uncertainty we'd rather avoid. However, if we wall ourselves off to adversity, we won't reap the benefits that an adverse situation can offer us.

We forget that adversity results in growth. It builds strength and character. It keeps your ego in check and reminds you that you aren't so different from anyone else. Adversity is also a wake-up call to revisit our bad habits, poor relationships, and how we spend our days.

These benefits only scratch the surface of adversity. What has adversity taught you in the past, and how will you face it when it comes calling again?

"Whatsoever thy hand findeth to do, do it with thy might."

—Ecclesiastes 9:10 (KJV)

Today's Anchor: The strongest people embrace adversity as a way to grow.

Winning the Ordinary Days

Getting Back on Track

Nothing feels better than getting back on track. The world will often seek to distract you and you may have no choice but to set aside time and effort to deal with those distractions. Quickly reset your mind and actions back in alignment with your personal and business goals.

If you're off course from where you want to go, remember that you always have choices on how to spend your time. You just need the discipline to adjust your thinking and actions.

Put yourself in a position to win by making sure you're doing the things you know that need to be done to win where it's the most important to you.

> *"Thus saith the LORD, Stand ye in the ways, and see, and ask for the old paths, where is the good way, and walk therein, and ye shall find rest for your souls."*
>
> *—Jeremiah 6:16 (KJV)*

Today's Anchor: You will face distractions and delays. Deal with them as quickly as possible.

Unshakable Confidence

Framing the Loop in Your Head

Loops of recurring thoughts in your head can be a blessing or a curse.

The best way to control them is by paying close attention to what we feed them because that is what they will speak back to us. It's not easy to master this, but it is possible when we use discipline to ensure what we're telling ourselves is helpful, kind, and truc to ourselves.

Use those pillars as a compass for your thoughts and know that when helpful, kind, and true are repeated internally, it is also what you repeat externally.

"Looking unto Jesus the author and finisher of our faith . . ."

—Hebrews 12:2 (KJV)

Today's Anchor: Anchor yourself in framing and let the rest fall into place.

Building a Life That Lasts

Working for a Larger Cause

Working together for a cause larger than ourselves should be our motivating purpose.

When we only do for ourselves, we receive limited rewards. When we do for shared purpose and one another, we are rewarded with so much more than we ask for.

Attack today with purpose for something bigger than you. Think of it as a mountain that you climb together, and one that you could never reach the peak if you attempted to climb it alone.

> *"And Jesus said unto him, No man, having put his hand to the plough, and looking back, is fit for the kingdom of God."*
>
> *—Luke 9:62 (KJV)*

Today's Anchor: Make your work personal.

Asking the Right Questions

When Things Are Beyond Your Control

When things happen outside of your control, and don't fit the perception of a plan you envisioned, you must take stock.

Can you take ownership for previous actions that produced a different path from what you want now? What can you learn that you can apply going forward? What will you do different if you get another chance at the same thing again?

When you don't stop and analyze outcomes that are different from what you want, you miss out on a critical step to improve your situation.

"Thou wilt shew me the path of life: in thy presence is fulness of joy; at thy right hand there are pleasures for evermore."

—Psalm 16:11 (KJV)

Today's Anchor: Learn to let go.

What This Week Changed in Me

From Weakness to Strength

Acknowledging where we are weak creates the greatest opportunity for strength. This requires awareness, honesty, and input from others, admitting we must continue to work on our shortcomings after we know what they are.

When we don't take time to do this, weaknesses undermine our confidence, and without it, we limit our ability to find growth that can turn a weakness into strength.

What do you need to acknowledge, seek counsel, and take action to strengthen your confidence and reduce weaknesses today?

> *"Humble yourselves therefore under the mighty hand of God, that he may exalt you in due time:"*
>
> *—1 Peter 5:6 (KJV)*

Today's Anchor: Identify your weaknesses, work on them, and soon they will turn to strengths.

Weekly Reflection:

____

____

____

____

____

____

Week 22

Staying the Course

The Rush to Judge Others

Why are we so quick to judge others, yet we are often slow to judge things we have done?

We must give ourselves a gentle reminder each time we are quick to do so. It's essential to remind ourselves we are not so different from others and that less judgment is a more peaceful and thoughtful way to live.

Nobody lives a perfect life, including you, so being quick to judge can be a dangerously ignorant and foolish way to treat others.

Often it's better to avoid pointing fingers unless you are looking in a mirror. Even then, think before you do. Give yourself the benefit of a doubt so that you can remain at peace with who you want to be.

"Walk humbly with thy God."

—Micah 6:8 (KJV)

Today's Anchor: Judge yourself the same way you judge others.

Strength Through the Struggle

Accept Reality

Accept what is, instead of pushing back against the fabric of what was meant to be.

Reality checks are hard but necessary to keep us on track and to save time by refusing to use energy that will not change an outcome, especially things that we can't control.

The sooner we accept what is, the sooner we can push through what was expected that we did not achieve. Wise people take lessons from this experience and to learn and grow into something amazing.

The pain is temporary but combined with glory that is held tightly in our hearts, they work together to create something special, if we allow them to do so.

> *"And not only so, but we glory in tribulations also: knowing that tribulation worketh patience;"*
>
> —*Romans 5:3 (KJV)*

Today's Anchor: Accept reality even when it is not favorable for you.

Winning the Ordinary Days

The Power of Leaning In

Stay focused and lean in, especially with the complex. Do not allow complacency or a shallow-minded approach to send you down the wrong path. That's why you must frequently ask yourself what areas are you allowing to plateau your progress?

Diligently pursuing what we want means sacrificing time and effort on things that matter less. This should not trouble you. Instead, you should celebrate that you are on the right path and taking important steps by leaning in daily to what matters most.

> *"He that tilleth his land shall have plenty of bread: but he that followeth after vain persons shall have poverty enough."*
>
> *—Proverbs 28:19 (KJV)*

Today's Anchor: Complacency kills progress; move through it.

Unshakable Confidence

Removing Fear

What would you do if you didn't have the ability to feed into your fears? Go a step further and ask yourself what good fear-based decisions have you made, and how did they turn out?

Fear is a limiting mindset. It is always good to approach your challenges by weighing all options. But when fear is at the top of the list, you have made your task much harder to accomplish.

But the more fear retreats in all parts of your life, the more you will experience bigger wins and greater peace.

"I will fear no evil: for thou art with me . . ."

—Psalm 23:4 (KJV)

Today's Anchor: When you are fearful, do that hard thing anyway.

Building a Life That Lasts

Acknowledging What We Want

One of the most important keys to change is acknowledging what we want. When we keep things to ourselves, we may be highly motivated, but without supporters, the path forward is more difficult.

Once we couple awareness with desire, we'll find out who our supporters are and if we're passionate enough to see things through to a successful completion.

> *"Commit thy way unto the LORD; trust also in him; and he shall bring it to pass."*
>
> *—Psalm 37:5 (KJV)*

Today's Anchor: Turn acknowledging into a decision, not a discussion.

Asking the Right Questions

What Thoughts Don't Serve You Well?

Is your brain cluttered with thoughts that don't serve you now or are impeding your future? Do these thoughts create a burden that you can do without?

Focusing on the present with gratitude coupled with disciplines and consistency will drown out thoughts that aren't helpful. You can be tactical with your thoughts.

To do so, ask yourself these questions: Does this serve me? What am I grateful for in the present moment? What intrusive thoughts do I need to own to move forward?

> *"The steps of a good man are ordered by the LORD: and he delighteth in his way."*
>
> *—Psalm 37:23 (KJV)*

Today's Anchor: Editing your thoughts is a key to a healthy life.

What This Week Changed in Me

Collaborating with Humble People

The most productive and happiest relationships come from collaborating with the humble. They do not allow egos to influence who they are and their calm demeanor always spreads to others.

Learn to spot those who practice humility in their personal and professional lives. They are stable and reliable, comfortable with who they are, and without an agenda that will derail results when you partner with them.

> *"Let nothing be done through strife or vainglory; but in lowliness of mind let each esteem other better than themselves. Look not every man on his own things, but every man also on the things of others."*
>
> *—Philippians 2:3–4 (KJV)*

Today's Anchor: Choose collaborating over comfort and watch what changes.

Weekly Reflection:

Week 23

Staying the Course

Pushing Through It

You will run up against times when you simply don't want to take on the tasks in front of you. But if you want to succeed, this is when you must apply maximum effort to push through your lack of desire.

You must make this pact with yourself and then keep it. Fill your mind with the fuel needed to persevere in small things and you will condition it to take on the large ones, too.

"Ponder the path of thy feet, and let all thy ways be established."

—Proverbs 4:26 (KJV)

Today's Anchor: Adversity is the best teacher to show us who we truly are.

Strength Through the Struggle

Accepting Criticism

When you change the course of your life and create new habits that serve you best, you may be criticized by others. Although you're ready to change and grow, they may not be in the same place. This should not deter you. Observe their feelings but stay the course.

Redefining those relationships is a necessary part of change. Either they will understand this or they will serve as reminders of why you needed to create a new standard in the first place.

What was once a comfortable relationship can quickly change to discomfort for others as you pursue new things. Remember that their discomfort is not your business. It's theirs to own, just like your new paths in life are yours to own.

> *"Turn not to the right hand nor to the left: remove thy foot from evil."*
>
> —*Proverbs 4:27 (KJV)*

Today's Anchor: Don't overcomplicate accepting criticism. It's necessary.

Winning the Ordinary Days

The Power of Continual Growth

When you attempt new things, you stretch in ways far beyond who you have been to that point. This growth creates a new baseline, unlocking the doors we want to open. As we unlock these doors, we discover new ones.

It takes time to understand that walking through many doors and accepting why others are closed is the secret to continual growth. But with enough practice and experience, we begin to more fully understand how continual growth is healthy and one of the best ways to guide us to a joyful life.

> *"The soul of the sluggard desireth, and hath nothing: but the soul of the diligent shall be made fat."*
>
> *—Proverbs 13:4 (KJV)*

Today's Anchor: Power comes from continually challenging growth.

Unshakable Confidence

Listening to Your Inner Voice

What you say to yourself matters more than what others say about you. Whether we say we can or can't do, we are right. And what we think we're worthy or capable of propels us in the direction where our mind points us.

Other's voices and opinions, which we can't control, are often biased and not accurate. Plus, we have no control over them. Instead, give the most attention to the encouragement and power you bring to yourself.

> *"The blessing of the LORD, it maketh rich, and he addeth no sorrow with it."*
>
> *—Proverbs 10:22 (KJV)*

Today's Anchor: Anchor yourself in listening within.

Building a Life That Lasts

Collaboration Is Magic

Giving others what they want and receiving what you need is how that magic is made. Support and gratitude changes the game and gives you the advantage to achieve the best outcomes. When you have a team aligned in a single direction, anything is possible. When you help others achieve their goals, you will win as well.

Being useful and collaborative is a choice that attracts like-minded people. It is better to operate in a positive, win-win environment where you will enjoy the process as much as the outcome.

> *"Without counsel purposes are disappointed: but in the multitude of counsellors they are established."*
>
> *—Proverbs 15:22 (KJV)*

Today's Anchor: Make collaboration personal and you are well on the way to ensuring everyone wins.

Asking the Right Questions

Do You Embrace Your Superpowers?

What are your God-given superpowers? Have you stopped to think about what they are and how you should use them to your advantage?

We all have clearly defined strengths that others may struggle with. We can use them to win by creating situations that play into our advantages. But we must fully understand what our advantages are.

Do not let your superpowers go unused. They are our duty to ourselves and our gift to help others.

> *"There are many devices in a man's heart; nevertheless the counsel of the LORD, that shall stand."*
>
> *—Proverbs 19:21 (KJV)*

Today's Anchor: Think about the special and unique gifts God has given you.

What This Week Changed in Me

Doing for Others as a Priority

Putting the needs of others first aligns you with the best parts of the universe. The gifts of kindness, humility, and caring are embraced as you focus less on yourself.

Placing our needs above others is selfish and inflates our ego, greed, and other parts of us that are often borne from fear and scarcity instead of abundance and love.

Do for others as you would want others to do for you. That sharing comes back to you many times over, often in surprising and joyful ways.

How can you help others today in unexpected ways that they won't see coming? In what ways can you selflessly place their needs above your own?

> *"And as ye would that men should do to you, do ye also to them likewise."*
>
> —*Luke 6:31 (KJV)*

Today's Anchor: Generosity is the fuel that propels a life well lived.

Weekly Reflection:

____

____

____

____

____

____

Week 24

Staying the Course

The Relationship Between Commitment and Growth

Commitment and growth work in unison. Before you can see growth, you must commit to overcome resistance and struggles that are common at the start of anything worthwhile. Struggles will try to defeat you, but those difficulties are exactly what you need to achieve breakthrough growth.

Most will want to retreat right as the transformation is happening, but growth is reserved for the few who persevere. Growth is not easy, but those willing to consistently pay the price will find ambitions will pair with actions to create incredible results.

> "*. . . meditate therein day and night . . . for then thou shalt make thy way prosperous, and then thou shalt have good success.*"
>
> —*Joshua 1:8 (KJV)*

Today's Anchor: To enjoy growth, you must commit to action.

Strength Through the Struggle

Removing Obstacles of Our Own Making

Sometimes we are our own worst enemies, creating barriers to success. We may do this unintentionally or it may be the result of a conscious choice. When this happens, do not allow it to grow, gain momentum, and become a habit.

This choice has always been ours but we must take conscious and directed steps to course correct when obstacles come to light.

What obstacle has become a habit you need to deal with today?

> *"For as he thinketh in his heart, so is he: Eat and drink, saith he to thee; but his heart is not with thee."*
>
> *—Proverbs 23:7 (KJV)*

Today's Anchor: Don't overcomplicate removing obstacles. Do what you already know to do.

Winning the Ordinary Days

The Right Way to Use Consistency

Consistency can be your greatest asset or your worst enemy, depending how you use it.

Before you push forward, make sure you are working on the right things for the right reasons. Your mission and purpose must align with consistent effort; otherwise, you will consistently work on the wrong things to earn payoffs you don't necessarily want.

Be truthful with yourself and you will find it easy to achieve consistency because you are invested in an outcome that matters to you.

> *"Let us hold fast the profession of our faith without wavering; for he is faithful that promised."*
>
> *—Hebrews 10:23 (KJV)*

Today's Anchor: Work on the right things for the right reasons.

Unshakable Confidence

Massive Momentum Starts with Instant Implementation

The key to massive momentum is instant implementation. For this to happen, you must have supreme confidence in your mission and direction. Armed with these things, you only hurt yourself when you procrastinate due to fear of failure or lack of time.

Momentum requires you to push through limiting beliefs and own the time and resources you need to conquer challenges. The only way you fail is when you don't act on something you desire. Challenge yourself to implement the things that are most important to you as soon as you can.

"Go to the ant, thou sluggard; consider her ways, and be wise."

—Proverbs 6:6 (KJV)

Today's Anchor: Remember, progress over perfection. Step into implementation even if you're not ready. You can adjust after you've started.

Building a Life That Lasts

Under Promise and Over Deliver

Under promising and over delivering is the simplest way to build repeatable business relationships.

In a world where we want to please everyone, we can find ourselves in a trap of falling short by setting the wrong expectations. Instead of worrying about securing business or completing a project, we maintain our integrity by having faith in what we can and cannot do within our means.

Knowing our capabilities and then consistently pushing ourselves to deliver levels beyond will create sustainable wealth for years to come.

> *"He that covereth his sins shall not prosper: but whoso confesseth and forsaketh them shall have mercy."*
>
> *—Proverbs 28:13 (KJV)*

Today's Anchor: Create added value by doing more than you say you will.

Asking the Right Questions

How Many Failures Do You Have in You?

What are the limits of the amount of failure you can withstand before you give up on something? There are limits attached to everything we attempt, but knowing you will lose or encounter setbacks along the way should be factored into any difficulty.

Do you understand by working toward success but allowing failure to be part of the process strengthens you immeasurably? Do you have a plan in place to use those failures to ultimately help you succeed?

If all you do is think about winning, but you don't factor in the ups and downs of that journey, you are making the journey more difficult.

The one who uses each failure to learn and fuel the end goal wins. How high can you raise the bar on your failure tolerance? That is the benchmark you need to overcome to become a better version of yourself.

> *"A faithful man shall abound with blessings: but he that maketh haste to be rich shall not be innocent."*
>
> *—Proverbs 28:20 (KJV)*

Today's Anchor: Embrace failure as a tool of growth.

What This Week Changed in Me

Authenticity Is Essential

Authenticity requires us to be vulnerable and expose our insecurities and shortcomings. However, when we have the courage to do this, we become unique and stand out from others who will hide who they truly are.

Instead of trying to fit in and be like everyone else, we should embrace our uniqueness. Doing so reveals our superpowers of who we are and what we choose to believe about ourselves.

When we live in this space, we show others who we really are, and in return, they can spot our authenticity and we amplify it to our advantage.

> *"Let love be without dissimulation. Abhor that which is evil; cleave to that which is good."*
>
> *—Romans 12:9 (KJV)*

Today's Anchor: Today, choose authenticity over comfort and watch what changes.

Weekly Reflection:

____

____

____

____

____

____

Week 25

Staying the Course

Stay Focused

Distractions are inevitable, and it's up to you to stay focused when they enter your life. Make this nonnegotiable when life throws everything at you that has nothing to do with your intentions.

Those who ignore what doesn't matter or align with their goals, and stay consistent with the plan they created, will win.

"*. . . that ye may attend upon the Lord without distraction.*"

—1 Corinthians 7:35 (KJV)

Today's Anchor: Stay focused no matter how many distractions you encounter. Take actions to remove them.

Strength Through the Struggle

Quieting the Unimportant Noise

When you get stuck reliving failures from your past, you negatively influence your future. If you aren't careful, unimportant thoughts and actions from your past will disrupt your life and place imaginary barriers in your way.

Know where these intrusive thoughts are coming from and shut them down as quickly as you can. Doing so gives you the time to regroup and refocus on the present.

You gain greater appreciation for the present when you no longer must battle things that do not serve you.

> *"Blessed is the man that walketh not in the counsel of the ungodly, nor standeth in the way of sinners, nor sitteth in the seat of the scornful."*
>
> *—Psalm 1:1 (KJV)*

Today's Anchor: Figure out what's important and let go of the rest.

Winning the Ordinary Days

Be Cautious with Your Consistency

Consistency is critical to long-term success. However, this assumes you consistently do the things that serve you best.

It's easy to fall back into habits that bring comfort but do not align with your goals. Working daily on habits that are misguided or not challenging enough to grow is nothing but wasted time.

Consistently implementing poor habits creates a dangerous place of consistent mediocrity.

Always be ready to course correct, even if it puts you in an uncomfortable place. Do the things that you have avoided but that now align with the results you desire. Let your actions meet your ambitions instead of falling into the trap of complacency.

"He that tilleth his land shall be satisfied with bread . . ."

—Proverbs 12:11 (KJV)

Today's Anchor: Protect discipline by protecting your standards.

Unshakable Confidence

Have Confidence in Your Faith

Living by your faith is noble, but living by it is not enough. You must put your faith into action.

Waiting for things to unfold without any implementation of what's been given isn't faith, it's complacency. This is a false interpretation of faith, thinking that your belief in God will be enough.

Your faith must bolster your confidence that you are doing the right things for the right reasons. But you must put that belief to work by doing what needs to be done to move things forward in the direction that aligns with your faith.

> *"Let the words of my mouth, and the meditation of my heart, be acceptable in thy sight, O LORD, my strength, and my redeemer."*
>
> *—Psalm 19:14 (KJV)*

Today's Anchor: Step into your faith to build confidence in your decisions.

Building a Life That Lasts

The Importance of Helping Others

Only good can come of something when you are doing it with the best of intentions for others.

It may not always be the expected result but if genuine care is the goal, then it will be the best one can expect.

Don't let the fear of failure stop you from moving toward the opportunities to serve others in life. Be the example and watch how others step up their game based on your willingness to help others.

"Bear ye one another's burdens, and so fulfil the law of Christ."

—Galatians 6:2 (KJV)

Today's Anchor: One of the most important things you can do is make the lives of others better.

Asking the Right Questions

What Fuels Your Passions?

What are the things in your life that excite you? When you wake up in the morning, what do you look forward to in your work, personal life, and relationships? When was the last time you fully leaned into what brings you joy?

If it's been a while, stop for a moment and be good to yourself by committing to what you're passionate about. Aside from feeling good, you'll also see tremendous growth because you're happy and inspired where you're at.

Keep your eye on your passions and make sure they are getting the attention they deserve. Mastery comes from fueling those fires not letting them burn out.

> *"Delight thyself also in the LORD; and he shall give thee the desires of thine heart."*
>
> *—Psalm 37:4 (KJV)*

Today's Anchor: Today, think about what you are most passionate about.

What This Week Changed in Me

The Proper Way to Think About Perception

Perception isn't reality unless we choose it to be. In a time when people quickly assume external projections are accurate, we must remind ourselves that it's our choice whether we buy into those perceptions or not.

We must remind ourselves that how we perceive the way we're living is only defined by the reality of if we're better off today than the day before. Do we have loving relationships? Are we growing more in our career?

Perception is often too focused on what others think about us instead of what we think about ourselves. When you turn this around and reflect on the type of life we're living instead of what other people think, we build value in who we are, which far outweighs the perception of their impressions.

> *"Be of good courage, and he shall strengthen your heart, all ye that hope in the LORD."*
>
> *—Psalm 31:24 (KJV)*

Today's Anchor: Your perception is a big part of your reality.

Weekly Reflection:

____

____

____

____

____

____

Week 26

Staying the Course

The Truth About Limiting Beliefs

Limiting beliefs are nothing more than thoughts implanted by others over a lifetime. These thought patterns can overwrite the reality we are all born with.

To erase limiting beliefs others have tried to impose on you, reset your mind to a limitless mindset through small daily actions that stack over time. When you catch yourself engaging in doubt or fear, tell yourself those thoughts are only illusions and not the reality that you deserve.

> *"A merry heart doeth good like a medicine: but a broken spirit drieth the bones."*
>
> *—Proverbs 17:22 (KJV)*

Today's Anchor: You are not required to entertain limiting thoughts and beliefs.

Strength Through the Struggle

You Will Fail Whether You Like It or Not

Failure is a part of success. You often try several approaches that won't produce the results you want until you hit on one that does.

Accepting failure as a stepping stone to success means you understand it can serve as an important tool that can grow you into a champion. No champion has become one without failure, nor will you. It's how you grow, learn, rise, and persevere with purpose.

> *"I waited patiently for the LORD; and he inclined unto me, and heard my cry."*
>
> *—Psalm 40:1 (KJV)*

Today's Anchor: There can be no meaningful successes without failures along the way.

Winning the Ordinary Days

Just Do It

When your vision is clear and your why is the fuel behind its purpose, be consistent in what needs to be done.

Don't delay or overthink it.

You know what needs to be done so just do it.

No excuses, complaining, or giving yourself a break.

You know what needs to be done so just do it.

Focus on pure, honest execution of the basic actions that produce momentum.

> *"Create in me a clean heart, O God; and renew a right spirit within me."*
>
> *—Psalm 51:10 (KJV)*

Today's Anchor: Take action and leave excuses behind.

Unshakable Confidence

Protect What You Feed Your Mind

Your mind pays close attention to what you feed it. This is critical because eventually it will feed back to you what you fed it in the first place.

Feed it criticism, doubt, and insecurity, and you will feel and express those things until you change your mental diet. Feed it positivity, conviction, and affirmation, and you will enjoy a meal of abundance later on.

Feeding your mind positivity does require work to control your thoughts. Be consistent and intentional in filling your mind with the right type of thoughts and you will enjoy the nourishment you want to achieve.

> *"Cast thy burden upon the LORD, and he shall sustain thee: he shall never suffer the righteous to be moved."*
>
> *—Psalm 55:22 (KJV)*

Today's Anchor: Filter what you tell your brain. Only allow the right kinds of thoughts in.

Building a Life That Lasts

The Transformation of Others

If you are filled with gratitude, then you will truly be excited as you watch others transform into the best versions of themselves. When you play a role in this change, it is often more fulfilling than the transformations in you.

Helping others is one of our highest callings. When you are in the habit of doing so, you have reached one of highest levels of compassion. As you help others grow, your actions will also transform you.

When your intentions are pure, your selfless actions will be rewarded in many ways.

> *"Give, and it shall be given unto you; good measure, pressed down, and shaken together, and running over . . . For with the same measure that ye mete withal it shall be measured to you again."*
>
> *—Luke 6:38 (KJV)*

Today's Anchor: Root hard for the changes for the better in others.

Asking the Right Questions

How Strongly Do You Rely on Your Convictions?

Are you convicted enough about who you are to use it as a powerful weapon to intentionally steer your life in the direction you want?

When you are full of conviction, you are selling yourself on the purpose for everything that you do. Is it possible for you to have this level of mental toughness and use it so that nothing can stop you? If not, what would it take to get to that level from where you're at now?

> *"For the LORD God is a sun and shield: the LORD will give grace and glory: no good thing will he withhold from them that walk uprightly."*
>
> —*Psalm 84:11 (KJV)*

Today's Anchor: Aligning path and purpose leads to strong conviction in your actions.

What This Week Changed in Me

Providing Value to Others

Value can be as simple as bringing someone something they never knew they needed. This may be as simple as reminding someone of something they already knew or offering a kind word of support during a friend or family member's difficult times.

When you are reluctant to share value with others by doing nothing in times of need, you diminish yourself as well. Keeping what you know and have to yourself is unnecessarily selfish.

Somedays your value will flow through to others effortlessly. Other days, you will need to dig deeper to bring it to the surface. The important thing is that you must care enough to share enough when it's needed.

> *"He that dwelleth in the secret place of the most High shall abide under the shadow of the Almighty."*
>
> *—Psalm 91:1 (KJV)*

Today's Anchor: Constantly look for ways to best serve others and place impact over income.

Weekly Reflection:

____

____

____

____

____

____

Week 27

Staying the Course

Don't Accept Delays

Use maximum effort to ensure there are no delays in the work you do. It's easy to find excuses and blame, but the fact is you can control actions and effort. Using outside forces to justify letting up because you're not fully committed is unacceptable.

Choosing complacency means that you are also making those choices in other areas. Decisions like this reveal your character, motivation, and the quality of life you want for you and your loved ones.

When you have a choice, choose action. Action is how you pay yourself with outsized returns that you can't fully see.

> *"Go to the ant, thou sluggard; consider her ways, and be wise: Which having no guide, overseer, or ruler, Provideth her meat in the summer, and gathereth her food in the harvest."*
>
> *—Proverbs 6:6–8 (KJV)*

Today's Anchor: Delays are a waste of time that you can never get back.

Strength Through the Struggle

Take Notes When You Fail

When you fail at a task, the best thing you can do is study why the failure happened and apply what you've learned to similar challenges in the future.

Failure is there to teach you what you need to know but you must be open to understanding what happened and what you must change. Use your experience to create expectations to excel later on. Don't miss the opportunity to give yourself feedback and create value from an outcome that didn't live up to your expectations.

> *"Though he fall, he shall not be utterly cast down: for the LORD upholdeth him with his hand."*
>
> *—Psalm 37:24 (KJV)*

Today's Anchor: Pay attention to how you fail and use it to learn going forward.

Winning the Ordinary Days

Consistency Requires Discipline; Discipline Requires Consistency

Consistency and discipline are two important traits that produce powerful results when closely aligned with each other. You must implement both to get outcomes that align with your long-term goals.

Outside forces will challenge these efforts daily. However, you must refocus your efforts when you encounter obstacles. Keeping your attention centered on what matters should not be negotiable and can be attained with persistence and perseverance.

> *"Whoso loveth instruction loveth knowledge: but he that hateth reproof is brutish."*
>
> —*Proverbs 12:1 (KJV)*

Today's Anchor: Consistency and discipline are critical tools you must use to enjoy success.

Unshakable Confidence

Mental Preparation Is Essential

It's easy to build on what you're familiar with, but to face tough challenges, you must prepare your weaknesses to make you a formidable opponent. This includes raising your mental and physical toughness so they're aligned.

It's impossible to dominate if you don't take preparation seriously. The battle is usually won before the fight starts. For this to happen, you must make sure your ambitions match your desired actions.

Set aside the time and resources you need to arm yourself. This is the way you show up, ready to engage in your peak state.

> *"I will lift up mine eyes unto the hills, from whence cometh my help. My help cometh from the LORD."*
>
> —*Psalm 121:1–2 (KJV)*

Today's Anchor: You must win the battle in your head before you can earn a victory on the field.

Building a Life That Lasts

Finish Strong

As you get closer to your goals, you may be tempted to let up a little as you start to celebrate your wins. This is a common mistake that is easily fixed if you keep telling yourself that there are no wins until you fully cross the finish line.

Keep your focus and discipline fully intact until the challenge in front of you is 100% complete. You may get bored with the mundane actions that put you in a position to win. However, doing these small and repetitive tasks consistently will produce the results for success instead of reasons for failure.

> *"Better is the end of a thing than the beginning thereof: and the patient in spirit is better than the proud in spirit."*
>
> —*Ecclesiastes 7:8 (KJV)*

Today's Anchor: You haven't scored a touchdown until you carry the ball into the end zone.

Asking the Right Questions

What Is Your Communication Style?

When you must share important information, how do you do it? Are you open and direct, concise and clear? Do you tailor the message to your audience and the situation? How would you rate yourself on your ability to deliver news, good or bad, in an honest and truthful manner?

To increase the chances for success, avoid setbacks, or creating enemies, you must avoid misunderstandings by embracing the correct way to approach the messages you want to convey. Respecting each other's communication style and being aware of potential faults in communicating saves time and headaches.

The best way to do this is to use your heart and head as a compass for your mouth.

> *"Let no corrupt communication proceed out of your mouth, but that which is good to the use of edifying, that it may minister grace unto the hearers."*
>
> —*Ephesians 4:29 (KJV)*

Today's Anchor: Words, body language, and tone matter. Pay attention to these things as you communicate with others.

What This Week Changed in Me

Embrace the Unknown

Don't fear what you don't know or understand. Instead, encourage your mind and body to venture into the unknown. Find new things that excite you and help you grow.

Push through the fear to build confidence that you can tackle more challenging and complex situations. Raise the bar to new heights and continually try to jump over it. This is how you create a new level beyond what is known and comfortable.

Treat confidence in exploring the unknown as the performance fuel you need to help you blast through fear and discomfort.

"This is the way, walk ye in it."

—Isaiah 30:21 (KJV)

Today's Anchor: Never be afraid of the parts of a situation you don't fully understand yet.

Weekly Reflection:

____

____

____

____

____

____

Week 28

Staying the Course

Pay Close Attention to Who Supports You

Not everyone around you will support your growth. Change is hard and it scares people who are not ready for it, whether in their own life or in yours.

When you change others may feel insecure and seek to keep you the way you are now. You must decide to manage their fears or ignore them completely because their thoughts are not yours to own.

Stay your course of truth toward the direction you are rising. Let no one hold you back to their standard while you create your own.

"Blessed is the man that trusteth in the LORD."

—Jeremiah 17:7 (KJV)

Today's Anchor: People who support you the most are people you must find a place for in your future.

Strength Through the Struggle

Know What Your Baseline Is

Never lose sight of your personal baseline. If you get too far off track from your goals and ambitions, it's critical to reset your life by returning to your baseline to get you back on track.

There are so many distractions and false information floating around that can easily undermine the habits that serve us. Everyone goes through periods like this and instead of beating yourself up when this happens, remove negative feelings and get back on track as quickly as you can.

"*I thought on my ways, and turned my feet unto thy testimonies.*"

—*Psalm 119:59 (KJV)*

Today's Anchor: Your baseline is the standard you use to grow from.

Winning the Ordinary Days

The Power of Momentum

Forward momentum is a series of small actions that accumulate over time. The more you gather, the more you build on them. The less you gather, the longer it takes. Remember, however, it's God's timing.

Stop trying to make things happen before their time. Do your part in the small actions and leave the results to Him.

> *"Man's goings are of the LORD; how can a man then understand his own way?"*
>
> —*Proverbs 20:24 (KJV)*

Today's Anchor: Stack the small steps. God can do more with steady progress than sudden pressure.

Unshakable Confidence

Trust Your Path

Unless you are filled with confidence, trusting yourself and your initial intentions can be challenging. To get over this hurdle, remind yourself of why you dedicated your time and efforts to your original goal in the first place.

Learn to trust yourself and you will stay on course and run a better race. The goals of a person should be treated like blinders on a horse.

Wear them with confidence in your mission, run a race at full speed, and cross the finish line as a winner.

> *"Trust in the LORD with all thine heart; and lean not unto thine own understanding."*
>
> *—Proverbs 3:5 (KJV)*

Today's Anchor: You can't trust others until you trust yourself first.

Building a Life That Lasts

Growing Knowledge Is Growing Wealth

To grow, you must constantly expand your knowledge. Make the pursuit of educating yourself intentional and automatic. Cultivate curiosity, ask questions, and seek wisdom.

Empty the mind of useless opinions, false information, and mental garbage, and refuel it with fresh ideas to expand what's possible. In this way, when you expand possibilities, you also expand the potential for wealth.

Combining what's tried and true with what's right and new will enable you to push your greatness even further.

> *"Ask, and it shall be given you; seek, and ye shall find; knock, and it shall be opened unto you:"*
>
> —*Matthew* 7:7 *(KJV)*

Today's Anchor: Knowledge leads directly to power and wealth.

Asking the Right Questions

What Frustrates You?

When frustrations rear up, can you see the connection between them and reflections of who you are? Do you understand that your values and hypocrisy determine the degree of frustration you have in other people and situations?

For example, if you value punctuality, and someone you depend on always runs late, does that feed into your frustrations? Of course it does. But have you also not been late?

When you are honest with what you value and how important it is to you, it is possible to better understand the source of your frustrations. If you can pinpoint the source of your frustrations, it might be easier for you to live in peace and harmony knowing that all our values differ.

What frustrates you today? And how will you deal with it going forward?

> *"Take my yoke upon you, and learn of me; for I am meek and lowly in heart: and ye shall find rest unto your souls."*
>
> *—Matthew 11:29 (KJV)*

Today's Anchor: Keep your cool even when events frustrate you.

What This Week Changed in Me

Daydreaming Is Healthy

Taking time to reflect on what's working and what's not while making adjustments to course correct on a regular basis is essential.

Giving yourself time to imagine possibilities and more efficient ways of doing things is a necessary and productive use of your time. Although it's impossible to quantify the act of daydreaming, understand the value of giving your brain and imagination the space it needs to work things out on your behalf.

Either they become allies in your new way of moving forward or you must take steps to remove their impacts on your life.

> *"Then said Jesus unto his disciples, If any man will come after me, let him deny himself, and take up his cross, and follow me."*
>
> *—Matthew 16:24 (KJV)*

Today's Anchor: Daydreaming opens the door to big possibilities.

Weekly Reflection:

____

____

____

____

____

____

Week 29

Staying the Course

Digging Deeper When You're Tired

When you're tired and don't see the results of the hard work you've put into a project, you may be tempted to ease up or quit. Many people do, but don't let that be you.

Instead, put aside your doubts and distractions. Focus on why you started your project in the first place. Then summon what energy you have, raise your mental toughness, and dig in even more.

As you move forward, celebrate your wins but also celebrate the fact that you didn't quit, because quitting would have been the easy thing to do. Work hard, evolve, grow, and succeed.

> *"For consider him that endured such contradiction of sinners against himself, lest ye be wearied and faint in your minds."*
>
> *—Hebrews 12:3 (KJV)*

Today's Anchor: You will learn much about who you are when you push the limits of who you think you are.

Strength Through the Struggle

Seeking Proactive Growth

Growth is an important part of life but it's too easy to fall into a place of comfort and ignore its necessity. We tend to endure enough pain to spur us to change instead of proactively looking for areas we can grow.

Our ego will play tricks on us, telling us we are good as is. It holds us back and provides a false sense of security instead of getting out of the way so we can move to bigger and better things.

Look at yourself daily and ask where and how you can grow, then take a step in that direction.

> *"Therefore I say unto you, What things soever ye desire, when ye pray, believe that ye receive them, and ye shall have them."*
>
> *—Mark 11:24 (KJV)*

Today's Anchor: Take the world by storm instead of letting the good eventually find its way to you.

Winning the Ordinary Days

The Best Use of Momentum

Momentum can be a blessing or a curse. When we use it to work on high-value projects, the ongoing energy works in our favor. When we use it on projects that are not a good use of our time and resources, we steer ourselves further away from where we want to be.

Before we can use momentum effectively, we must give serious thought to how we spend our time. Acknowledge and test where you want to apply your energy, and then consistently apply it to create important momentum that intentionally advances the right things.

> *"In the morning sow thy seed, and in the evening withhold not thine hand . . ."*
>
> —*Ecclesiastes 11:6 (KJV)*

Today's Anchor: Aim your energy at what matters most. Momentum is powerful when pointed in the right direction.

Unshakable Confidence

Decide and Act

Making the decision to be the best version of yourself should be your main priority.

Starting there affects all other decisions. It builds a formidable mindset that enables you to persevere through whatever is thrown at you.

Use this thinking to give everything you have to support your mission. If you fall short from the results you wanted, you can still feel good that you gave everything you had.

Never become complacent, wondering what might have been.

> *"How long halt ye between two opinions? if the LORD be God, follow him: but if Baal, then follow him."*
>
> *—1 Kings 18:21 (KJV)*

Today's Anchor: Be decisive every chance you get.

Building a Life That Lasts

The Importance of a Proactive Plan

To succeed, you must create a road map of your future. If you don't know exactly where you want to go and how you're going to get there, you will stray from anything meaningful and wind up in places you don't want to go.

But the creation of a well-thought-out plan isn't enough. Your plan should excite you so that the outcome will bring you joy. You must also have action and accountability as part of the plan for success. If you don't combine planning, joy, action, and accountability, you'll only delay reaching your goal and the gratification that goes with it.

> *"The preparations of the heart in man, and the answer of the tongue, is from the LORD."*
>
> *—Proverbs 16:1 (KJV)*

Today's Anchor: Work hard now but always have an eye toward what comes next.

Asking the Right Questions

Attack Your Blind Spots

Do you have weaknesses and blind spots that are holding you back from what you want to accomplish? Are there reasons why you allow these things to exist when you know your life would be better if they were handled properly?

Aside from the grace, discipline, and consistency, what other tools and character traits must you have to succeed?

The most important of these is discipline. It is what makes all other actions possible. This is why a path of discipline leads to more discipline and you must welcome it if you're fully committed to your goals.

"Let the weak say, I am strong."

—Joel 3:10 (KJV)

Today's Anchor: Today, think about how you can turn weaknesses into strengths.

What This Week Changed in Me

Replacing Old Habits with New

As we build a foundation of new habits, we will find the old ones less attractive than they once were. This is a sign of growth and we should seek these new habits as often as possible.

Equally important, as you discover new ways to live, remember to not allow the old habits to take root again. Creating new habits can be uncomfortable, and if we're not fully committed, it's easy for the false comfort of old habits to return and deceive you into believing this is where you should put your energy.

> *"But put ye on the Lord Jesus Christ, and make not provision for the flesh, to fulfil the lusts thereof."*
>
> *—Romans 13:14 (KJV)*

Today's Anchor: As you grow, new habits must replace what no longer works.

Weekly Reflection:

____

____

____

____

____

____

Week 30

Staying the Course

Stacking Small Wins Accumulates over Time

Taking small steps daily toward a worthy goal may not feel like much. But over the long haul, these tiny efforts create an ongoing momentum that feed into our big purpose.

When you can't see this, you're more inclined to give up because you can't see how momentum swings efforts in your favor.

You must also consider that momentum and forward progress are part of God's timing. You can chip away daily but keep in mind that results will not happen before their time. Stop trying to force things to happen. Do your part with small and continuous momentum and leave the end results up to Him.

> *"What shall we then say to these things? If God be for us, who can be against us?"*
>
> —*Romans 8:31 (KJV)*

Today's Anchor: Momentum compounds success over time.

Strength Through the Struggle

Finding a Clear Direction Isn't Always Easy

You will be pulled in many directions as you navigate through life. At times, you may feel overwhelmed and that pressure will cause you to go in the direction of what is familiar, not what is best. While the familiar got you to where you are today, it may no longer serve where you want to go now.

When you feel confused and overloaded, take a step back and remind yourself of where you want to go and why. After doing this, if you still find the familiar is what works best for you, then you can proceed with confidence and alignment knowing how you'll make the most progress on your goals.

> *"Shew me thy ways, O LORD; teach me thy paths. Lead me in thy truth, and teach me: for thou art the God of my salvation; on thee do I wait all the day."*
>
> *—Psalm 25:4–5 (KJV)*

Today's Anchor: Don't get discouraged when it takes time to discover the right path.

Winning the Ordinary Days

The Fuel of Daily Intention

You can do anything you put your mind to but you must approach these challenges with a plan and daily intentions; otherwise, you won't get far. Consistently thinking about how to execute your plans starts with want and will, but it is the plans you put into action that push you forward to what you want to do.

Focus on the right kind of intention to optimize your actions that can take you anywhere. You may need tenacity, wisdom, patience, greater knowledge, or other critical elements to drive you. Whatever those fuels may be, it's important to consistently tap into them as your goals and efforts take shape.

> *"Walk in wisdom toward them that are without, redeeming the time."*
>
> —*Colossians 4:5 (KJV)*

Today's Anchor: Use intention as you would use the rudder of a boat.

Unshakable Confidence

Being Decisive

You are often called on to make decisions quickly and accurately. This can be uncomfortable when you want more information or time to make up your mind. Those are luxuries leaders rarely get a chance to use.

Instead, you must sharpen adjacent skills regularly. These include learning to read people, looking for underlying motives, and figuring out what others want from you.

Life is such that you don't always get to wait for the right time or conditions. Instead, when you're able to quickly understand what's really going on, you can reach decisions that advance what you want far greater.

> *"Choose you this day whom ye will serve . . . but as for me and my house, we will serve the LORD."*
>
> —*Joshua 24:15 (KJV)*

Today's Anchor: Decisive actions remove pain and create clear paths to victories.

Building a Life That Lasts

Drawing on the Knowledge of Others

A smart person knows they don't have all the answers. But if you are a truly wise person, you will understand that you must seek out others who have already traveled where you want to go.

Relying on that experience and knowledge saves time, money, and the threat of going in the wrong direction with unnecessary costs that could have been avoided.

Do not allow pride and ego to get in the way. They will only make things more difficult before you realize you need help to get back on the best path forward.

> *"For by wise counsel thou shalt make thy war: and in multitude of counsellors there is safety."*
>
> *—Proverbs 24:6 (KJV)*

Today's Anchor: Accept that you don't know everything and seek others to help you fill in the gaps.

Asking the Right Questions

How Big Is Your Vision?

People often don't dream big enough out of fear or the potential for failure. Are you one of these people? If so, why? What's holding you back? What are you afraid of? What's the worst that could happen?

This is how you put things into perspective. On the flip side, you must also ask yourself how your life will change for the better if you do the work and your dreams come true. Are you excited for that answer? Are you ready to do what it takes to succeed? On a fundamental level, do you know what it will take?

What if you went many steps beyond what you could imagine? Are your visions and dreams big enough to create the life you really want? Or are you playing it safe, refusing to venture too far because it scares you too much?

Until you overcome this fear, you will be stuck in a lesser life than you deserve.

> *"And God is able to make all grace abound toward you; that ye, always having all sufficiency in all things, may abound to every good work:"*
>
> *—2 Corinthians 9:8 (KJV)*

Today's Anchor: Do you dream big enough?

What This Week Changed in Me

Seek Guidance Before You Act

Routinely seek the advice of others who are more experienced than you. Listen closely, weigh your options, and then act to avoid becoming paralyzed by fear of the outcome.

The direction you plan to go means nothing when you stay neutral. Based on what you have learned, you must put that knowledge to work. Do not fear outcomes because they are also useful to help you course correct and guide you toward the best possible outcome. It is not helpful to be given directions but then never move forward in a direction meant for you.

> *"Where no counsel is, the people fall: but in the multitude of counsellors there is safety."*
>
> *—Proverbs 11:14 (KJV)*

Today's Anchor: Rely on others you trust to guide you before you act.

Weekly Reflection:

____

____

____

____

____

____

Week 31

Staying the Course

Getting Stuck in Familiar Ways

Sometimes you get stuck in familiar ways of doing things and don't pay attention to the fact that your habits and processes no longer serve you. If your life is busy and full, it's easy to become inefficient instead of actively seeking ways to shed yourself from that which no longer works in your favor.

A better approach is to stay mindful of how you spend your time and effort. Don't dwell on the past. Instead, focus on the future and decide what you need to keep moving forward. Be relentless in using personal insights to put you on track to a happier and more productive life.

> *"Finally, my brethren, be strong in the Lord, and in the power of his might."*
>
> *—Ephesians 6:10 (KJV)*

Today's Anchor: The familiar old ways can be a trap if you stay with them too long.

Strength Through the Struggle

Complexity Versus Simplicity

You can often achieve the same results with a simple approach to problems instead of getting worked up about complicated solutions that usually requires more time, money, and energy.

Learn to approach your problems with a basic mindset, filtering in the tools and strategies you need to solve them.

Stay with what you know. Ask questions and seek answers, but in general, most answers are clear if you know how and where to look for them.

> *"Let nothing be done through strife or vainglory; but in lowliness of mind let each esteem other better than themselves."*
>
> *—Philippians 2:3 (KJV)*

Today's Anchor: Complicating things is usually not a good path to achieving great results.

Winning the Ordinary Days

Using Leverage to Your Advantage

Consistently leveraging systems and teams to execute plans is a recipe for success.

When we do things without a clear purpose and end goal, we lack motivation to stay on course, and drift needlessly. Taking actions systematically and putting them in place with the help of others leverages the chance for repeating results we desire.

> *"Moreover thou shalt provide out of all the people able men, such as fear God, men of truth, hating covetousness; and place such over them, to be rulers of thousands, and rulers of hundreds, rulers of fifties, and rulers of tens."*
>
> *—Exodus 18:21 (KJV)*

Today's Anchor: Leverage is an important tool to stack the odds in your favor.

Unshakable Confidence

The Right Kind of Self-Talk

The messages you feed into your brain and what it repeats back to you must be carefully managed. You must set aside opinions, irrational thoughts, and noise that doesn't matter.

Instead focus on facts, positive affirmations, and how you're using this to inspire others.

The right kind of self-talk can build your confidence instead of tearing it down. Speaking to others can do the same, but it all starts inside.

Pay attention to those little voices in your head. If they get out of line, don't tolerate their existence. Ignite the flames of success instead of dousing your dreams in a bottomless well of poor self-talk.

"Set your affection on things above, not on things on the earth."

—Colossians 3:2 (KJV)

Today's Anchor: Speak kindly and lovingly to yourself today.

Building a Life That Lasts

Finding Prosperity in the Here and Now

Finding ways that fill the heart and mind starts in the present moment. When we search for fulfillment from our past or look toward the future, we miss all that is in front of us now.

Be where your feet are, finding comfort in knowing that you are connected and secure exactly where you are supposed to be.

> *"Behold, I will rain bread from heaven for you; and the people shall go out and gather a certain rate every day ..."*
>
> —*Exodus 16:4 (KJV)*

Today's Anchor: You don't need to go far to find the gifts that are meant for you today.

Asking the Right Questions

Is Your Vision Big Enough?

Are you excited about growing into your future? Have you set a high standard and goals that get you fired up every day? If not, what's holding you back and why?

Do you battle enemies of insecurity and fear of the unknown? Have you downsized your big and bold ideas into something and with more chance of success? If so, why?

Until you step out and take a chance on things that seem impossible, you'll never know how talented you are and how far you can go.

"Enlarge the place of thy tent, and let them stretch forth the curtains of thine habitations: spare not, lengthen thy cords, and strengthen thy stakes;"

—Isaiah 54:2 (KJV)

Today's Anchor: Use vision to fuel your biggest dreams.

What This Week Changed in Me

How Committed Are You?

Mindset is everything, and until you are completely vested in believing you can win, you are creating doubt that makes winning more difficult.

Always remember you must be committed and truly believe you can win, not just interested in the possibility of winning, for the big opportunities that can change your life.

Reframe your mindset. What if you lifted the ceiling entirely on what you thought was possible and created a new one? Build on it and massage it until it scares you. That's how you turn big visions into reality.

> *"For we are made partakers of Christ, if we hold the beginning of our confidence stedfast unto the end;"*
>
> *—Hebrews 3:14 (KJV)*

Today's Anchor: Decide what you'll commit to today and move toward it with full intensity.

Weekly Reflection:

____

____

____

____

____

____

Week 32

Staying the Course

Faith Overcomes the Fear of Execution

Many times, we fight inner battles of doubt and self-worth. This affects our ability to drive past these fears that are often irrational.

To overcome these fears, we must allow faith to push those negatives aside. Faith creates momentum and progress. Faith destroys fear.

But the biggest benefit of all is that faith creates ongoing peace in our lives.

"Be not afraid, only believe."

—Mark 5:36 (KJV)

Today's Anchor: Today, choose faith over comfort and watch what changes.

Strength Through the Struggle

Falling Down Is Part of the Process

Failure and falling down are important parts of any worthy journey. When you encounter setbacks it forces you to decide if there is still value in pursuing your goal. Falling down also means the journey is challenging and is therefore a good use of your time. That's because all worthy challenges produce dramatic growth when framed the right way.

If you fall down, get up, dust yourself off, and decide how hard to chase after your goal. Simply keep in mind that with no pain, there is no change, and with no change there is no growth.

"Casting all your care upon him; for he careth for you."

—1 Peter 5:7 (KJV)

Today's Anchor: You can't get up stronger than you already are if you don't fall down along the way.

Winning the Ordinary Days

Habits That No Longer Serve Us Well

What habits do you continue with that don't serve you anymore? Have you taken a moment to reflect on why you allow them to remain in your life?

Some are comfortable, but not helpful. They show up unannounced and fall into parts of our day.

It's up to you to identify what those old habits are and replace them with more effective ones that serve you with a more meaningful purpose.

Create a new form of consistency by choosing this correction instead of remaining in chaotic outdated patterns.

> *"And have put on the new man, which is renewed in knowledge after the image of him that created him:"*
>
> —*Colossians 3:10 (KJV)*

Today's Anchor: Change out habits that no longer produce meaningful results.

Unshakable Confidence

Being Direct Lessens the Need to Persevere

When you are direct and honest with yourself, as tough as it can be, you are moving forward with difficult truths that require you to keep persevering. Excuses are wiped out in favor of progress, solutions, and ultimately the resolution of the challenges you are facing.

Part of this self-analysis means being open to creating action in ways that we may not have been comfortable doing in the past. It's the only way forward.

Falling back into patterns of doing what we once did will only get us so far. It can be directly opposed to evolving into a new and better version of who we are in life and business.

> "*. . . putting away lying, speak every man truth with his neighbour . . .*"
>
> —*Ephesians 4:25 (KJV)*

Today's Anchor: Eliminate unnecessary truths to clear the shortest path to your best life.

Building a Life That Lasts

The Lessons of Gratitude

Gratitude releases the soul from fear and anxiety. It is a mixture of peace, humility, kindness, and caring. Gratitude also creates awareness that increases the blessings inside of us.

Do you have enough gratitude in your life? What lessons has gratitude taught you? Find these answers and you will find deeper truths about who you are and how much you have already achieved.

"O give thanks unto the LORD; for he is good . . ."

—Psalm 136:1 (KJV)

Today's Anchor: Take note of the lessons you learn from practicing gratitude today.

Asking the Right Questions

Can You Keep It Simple?

Do you have a tendency to overthink things? Does this cause you anxiety and insecurity because you don't know which way to go? Do you have it within you to simplify things and consider their impacts on those terms?

Keeping it simple boils down to one question: What are you willing or unwilling to do each day?

If you're clear, then it becomes a battle of desire and discipline to take action.

Anything else is noise that complicates your decision. Tune that noise out and keep it simple if you want progress.

> *"A time to rend, and a time to sew; a time to keep silence, and a time to speak;"*
>
> —*Ecclesiastes 3:7 (KJV)*

Today's Anchor: Overthinking is a waste of time. Let it go and get on with things.

What This Week Changed in Me

Knowing the Value in Ourselves

We don't always need to provide value to others, but we must always understand the value we have in ourselves.

To be valuable we must be of value to others. At times, we can make the mistake of placing our own value with the value we provide to others.

We all want to feel valuable but must remember that our real value comes from God's eyes, not the eyes of others.

> *"For ye are bought with a price: therefore glorify God in your body, and in your spirit, which are God's."*
>
> *—1 Corinthians 6:20 (KJV)*

Today's Anchor: Believe in the power of you.

Weekly Reflection:

____

____

____

____

____

____

Week 33

Staying the Course

Trust the Process

Trusting in your process when things don't appear to be going your way is one of the hardest things to do. Remember that the process has been deliberately pointed at you and your goals for specific reasons. Some you may understand while others may be hidden beneath the surface and will reveal themselves later.

As you learn more about a situation, it's okay to modify your process to optimize your efforts. But this must be done with a clear mind and confidence that what you want is worthy of your time and effort. So, stay focused and keep moving forward.

> *"Teach me to do thy will; for thou art my God: thy spirit is good; lead me into the land of uprightness."*
>
> *—Psalm 143:10 (KJV)*

Today's Anchor: Processes and systems bring order and success to your life.

Strength Through the Struggle

Reframing Is an Important Strategy

Reframing your mind to seek the opportunity in a negative situation can be the difference between winning or losing.

Be mindful of how you perceive things and look for ways to flip weaknesses in your favor. Consider your options, ask for help, and weigh the implications of various paths forward.

> *"But as for you, ye thought evil against me; but God meant it unto good ..."*
>
> —*Genesis 50:20 (KJV)*

Today's Anchor: Changing your perspective is the first step to changing your life.

Winning the Ordinary Days

Enemy or Asset?

Consistency can be your greatest asset or your worst enemy.

Everyone is capable of implementing consistency in their lives. It requires discipline to use it the right way, for the right reasons, and in the right situations.

When you engage in a regular and productive use of your time and resources, you will get results that you and others can enjoy. Always be aware of how you can use consistency to your advantage and be on guard to not let it become an enemy by using it the wrong way.

> *"Whoso keepeth the commandment shall feel no evil thing: and a wise man's heart discerneth both time and judgment."*
>
> *—Ecclesiastes 8:5 (KJV)*

Today's Anchor: Ask yourself what your relationship is with consistency.

Unshakable Confidence

Believing in the Impossible

Believe in the impossible and watch the cage of limitations open.

It starts with the belief that anything is possible with God guiding you and others. When that belief becomes conviction, others will see it in you and follow. This shared vision tilts the scales in your favor, and soon enough, what seemed impossible can become a reality.

"For with God nothing shall be impossible."

—Luke 1:37 (KJV)

Today's Anchor: It's impossible only if you think it's impossible.

Building a Life That Lasts

The Gift of Another Chance

Far too often we take it for granted when we're given the gift of another chance.

What we do with them, how we respond, or whether we even notice them is up to us. You must be aware when God places these in your life and respond to these gifts by saying thank you for the gift if you choose to open it.

> *"Behold, I will do a new thing; now it shall spring forth; shall ye not know it?..."*
>
> —*Isaiah 43:19 (KJV)*

Today's Anchor: The gift of another chance to others is a gift rooted in your level of gratitude toward yourself.

Asking the Right Questions

The Pull of a Magnet

Are you attracting and using the tools that are in alignment with your vision?

Think of alignment as a magnet. There are two sides of a magnet and both can be uncomfortable but useful tools in helping you achieve your goal. Do you know how your magnets are pushing or pulling you? Are you positioning the magnets in your life so that they are correctly aligned with what you want to achieve?

It's not the magnet's fault for doing what it does naturally. It's up to you to place it correctly so that you get the push and pull benefits of a tool that is meant to help you.

> *"The wisdom of the prudent is to understand his way: but the folly of fools is deceit."*
>
> *—Proverbs 14:8 (KJV)*

Today's Anchor: Alignment is a magnet that attracts opportunities into your life.

What This Week Changed in Me

Putting Others First

Serving others as a priority expands our capacity for giving while creating proper alignment in our thinking. When we place our needs first, they are often driven by ego, greed, or fear, and we lose sight of the kind of success that matters most.

Make it a habit to do for others as you would want others for you. Do this and see over time how that comes back to you many times over.

What will you do for others today they never saw coming?

> *"My little children, let us not love in word, neither in tongue; but in deed and in truth."*
>
> *—1 John 3:18 (KJV)*

Today's Anchor: Lead with generosity; put someone else first today.

Weekly Reflection:

____

____

____

____

____

____

Week 34

Staying the Course

Find a Way to Get Back on Track

If you get distracted or have pulled away from your primary objectives, find a way to reset your priorities and how you allocate your time as soon as possible.

A good way to approach this is to remind yourself that you are in charge of where you place your effort. You can change directions at any time because you always have a choice.

Start today by asking what is the one thing you can do to get back on track and create a positive domino effect.

> *"I am the LORD thy God . . . which leadeth thee by the way that thou shouldest go."*
>
> —*Isaiah 48:17 (KJV)*

Today's Anchor: Don't beat yourself up for getting off track. Simply reset and get moving in the right direction again.

Strength Through the Struggle

Fighting Through Old Scripts

Fear of losing and not being enough are scripts that may have been implanted in you at an early age. You may not have been aware that these barriers were being passed on to you. They quietly lurk inside of you and can sabotage who you are now.

When you get angry or your ego attempts to defend you, this may be the result of old and limiting beliefs you have about yourself. Have you stopped to consider what untruths have been passed down to you and how they affect you today?

To combat these feelings, you must respond with love and compassion. This is how you break negative cycles so you can live without fear and pain, and instead live with love, compassion, and acceptance.

> *"Let not sin therefore reign in your mortal body, that ye should obey it in the lusts thereof."*
>
> —*Romans 6:12 (KJV)*

Today's Anchor: Sometimes your past is the biggest enemy you have.

Winning the Ordinary Days

Consistency Requires Discipline

Too often, we commit to daily habits and routines with good intentions, only to give up on our efforts after a short period of time. We begin with a strong-willed commitment to consistency but when we get discouraged, we abandon our efforts instead of applying more discipline.

Discipline is the key to consistency. It must work together with consistency to produce the kind of life-changing results you deserve. One without the other makes the journey much more difficult. Feeding them equally produces the accountability that creates infinite growth.

"The sluggard will not plow by reason of the cold . . ."

—Proverbs 20:4 (KJV)

Today's Anchor: Discipline is the key to accomplishing much in life.

Unshakable Confidence

Trust Is a Necessity

There is no replacement for trust in your life. When you demonstrate trust, you build confidence in other people. They have a clear understanding of who you are and what you want. This is accomplished by creating a track record of doing what you say you will do.

This is how you avoid confusion, lack of productivity, and problems while building a team that is fully focused on solutions.

> *"Death and life are in the power of the tongue: and they that love it shall eat the fruit thereof."*
>
> *—Proverbs 18:21 (KJV)*

Today's Anchor: Demonstrate trust and expect it in others.

Building a Life That Lasts

Tell Your Mind Where to Go

Your mind guides you and is a strong ally when you tell it to implement your plans in a bold and powerful way.

You decide what your mind should focus on and in what direction it goes. You decide whether to influence yourself and others. We cannot control many things but we can influence the quality of our actions with positive thinking.

Focus on powerful ideas and actions to produce good outcomes for you and others. Unleash your unlimited potential for selfless greatness. In this way you will produce tangible and intangible wealth that goes far beyond our limitations of time and effort when we focus only on ourselves.

> *"Also, that the soul be without knowledge, it is not good; and he that hasteth with his feet sinneth."*
>
> *—Proverbs 19:2 (KJV)*

Today's Anchor: Be intentional to find peace of mind in your actions.

Asking the Right Questions

Big Questions to Think About

What is the why that drives you? How well do others know this about you? How much difference would it make in your relationships if they did?

We spend too much time stuck in what we do that it's easy to forget why we do it. The why is what brings us peace, drives us, and creates relatability and authenticity.

Are you ready to tell the truth, especially to yourself?

> *"Counsel in the heart of man is like deep water; but a man of understanding will draw it out."*
>
> *—Proverbs 20:5 (KJV)*

Today's Anchor: Seek answers to big questions because your future is bigger than today's distraction.

What This Week Changed in Me

The Gift of Listening

When you engage in active listening, you not only invest in the originator of the message but also in the knowledge you're receiving. So often, we listen far below our capacity to fully seek knowledge from others. We are easily distracted or have predetermined ideas about what we want to hear or say.

This shuts out opportunities to grow and learn at a deeper level. Remain aware, be inquisitive, and ask questions that lead from one piece of information to the next.

> *"Be not rash with thy mouth, and let not thine heart be hasty to utter any thing before God ..."*
>
> *—Ecclesiastes 5:2 (KJV)*

Today's Anchor: Pick one behavior that honors the gift of listening and execute it.

Weekly Reflection:

____

____

____

____

____

____

Week 35

Staying the Course

Make Ongoing Adjustments

Even when things are working in your favor, you must look at the way in which they are working and be prepared to make adjustments for greater efficiencies.

Reevaluating your thoughts and processes is mandatory for advancing to the next level.

Make necessary course adjustments when you spot the need and remember even being one degree off over time will only ensure you arrive at the wrong destination.

> *"Seest thou a man diligent in his business? he shall stand before kings; he shall not stand before mean men."*
>
> —*Proverbs 22:29 (KJV)*

Today's Anchor: Flexibility in your approach is the way to advancing to the next level.

Strength Through the Struggle

The First Step Is the Hardest

You may be facing unpleasant tasks in your life or avoiding them. Rather than set these challenges aside, you must commit to taking a first step because it is the hardest part of the entire journey.

Each one thereafter will create new habits as you build toward mastery. Keep in mind that you are not born a master of a craft or skill. It's something that is built on day by day through study, practice, and consistency over time.

What is the first step you have been holding back from that will push you into the mastery that you have been searching for?

"For who hath despised the day of small things?..."

—Zechariah 4:10 (KJV)

Today's Anchor: Anchor yourself in a first step and let the rest fall into place.

Winning the Ordinary Days

When Consistency Is Not Consistent

You may sell yourself on the idea that doing things over the short term is an act of consistency. That's a nice story but it is not the definition of consistency.

The short term can build a solid foundation for consistency. But too often, we give up too soon when we don't see immediate results. We lack the discipline and mental toughness that is required to do hard things when we get discouraged. To be successful, consistency and discipline must work together.

> "*. . . give diligence to make your calling and election sure: for if ye do these things, ye shall never fall:*"
>
> —*2 Peter 1:10 (KJV)*

Today's Anchor: Understand that a series of actions in the short term does not equal consistency in the long term.

Unshakable Confidence

Receiving Feedback Is a Gift

Receiving feedback when you fall short of your full potential is one of the greatest gifts you can receive. Sometimes, you are too close to a situation and can't always see what others can. They are able to see things with less bias, and their clear-headed counsel adds unique perspective.

Build a network that you can rely on for feedback. Make sure their input advances your project with constructive input instead of criticizing it. Through the lens of others, you will gain new insights you can implement with renewed confidence.

> *"Make no friendship with an angry man; and with a furious man thou shalt not go: Lest thou learn his ways, and get a snare to thy soul."*
>
> —*Proverbs 22:24-25 (KJV)*

Today's Anchor: Don't defend, learn. Good feedback is a shortcut to growth.

Building a Life That Lasts

The Source of True Wealth

When you have a choice, help others before you help yourself. This act of kindness brings extreme value and satisfaction to our lives.

Often, it is the important stepping stone we need that brings us closer to having our wants and needs fulfilled. Part of the reason for this is that when we help others, there is a natural reciprocal act that happens because others will help you fulfill yours. But if you always put yourself first, you should also prepare for a long, lonely road ahead.

> *"He that hath pity upon the poor lendeth unto the LORD; and that which he hath given will he pay him again."*
>
> *—Proverbs 19:17 (KJV)*

Today's Anchor: The ability to give creates the ability to receive.

Asking the Right Questions

Do Not Overlook Your Inner Perseverance

We often overlook or discount the amount of perseverance we have. We don't give ourselves enough credit for the things we've successfully accomplished and our ability to stay on course despite setbacks that come our way.

Your ability to persevere is a catalyst for what comes next. Remember what you have accomplished thus far and keep building on your successes instead of discounting them.

> *"Many are the afflictions of the righteous: but the LORD delivereth him out of them all."*
>
> *—Psalm 34:19 (KJV)*

Today's Anchor: You have it in you to get through just about anything that is put in your way.

What This Week Changed in Me

What Would You Say About You Today?

Following a path into your future means going back to the version of ourselves that we are leaving behind. As we grow, we rely on our past experiences to guide us, especially when we were at the lowest points in our lives.

Occasionally revisiting our past and trying to gain insights is critical. The passage of time enables us to gain new perspectives and bring clarity to chapters we created and those who created chapters for us.

Digging deep for the lessons you may have left behind and adding them back will bring you joy as God intended.

> *"And said, Verily I say unto you, Except ye be converted, and become as little children, ye shall not enter into the kingdom of heaven."*
>
> *—Matthew 18:3 (KJV)*

Today's Anchor: Be proud of what you are now by looking back at what you were long ago.

Weekly Reflection:

____

____

____

____

____

____

Week 36

Staying the Course

Self-Discipline Requires Proper Motivation

When you want to be disciplined in your life, make sure the purpose and the payoff is large enough. You will find it much easier to do difficult things when they advance goals that matter most to you.

Visualizing outcomes and the benefits you'll enjoy when you complete a task make the implementation of self-discipline easier. When you are willing to wait for the best things in life, discipline serves you well, instead of being a barrier to how you want to live now.

> *"He that is slow to anger is better than the mighty; and he that ruleth his spirit than he that taketh a city."*
>
> *—Proverbs 16:32 (KJV)*

Today's Anchor: Make self-discipline personal for lasting changes.

Strength Through the Struggle

The Pros and Cons of Fight or Flight

Our fight-or-flight mode is a survival tool we use to excel in an area we usually wouldn't find ourselves. It is a useful warning system that protects us, but sometimes it kicks in at the wrong times.

When our brain misreads a situation, we can get stuck in this mode when it's not necessary.

While it can be effective weapon to protect us, it's highly dysfunctional when it disconnects us from our creativity and replaces it with anxiety.

We were never meant to live in a constant state of fight or flight. Harness it properly and use gratitude as the compass to stay grounded and in line with the mode God intended for our true self.

> *"Every word of God is pure: he is a shield unto them that put their trust in him."*
>
> *—Proverbs 30:5 (KJV)*

Today's Anchor: Know when to fight back and when to move on.

Winning the Ordinary Days

Choosing the Right Habits

Consistency of habits is the key to success. But you must choose the right habits; otherwise, you will burn up a lot of energy and waste time.

Too often we convince ourselves what we are consistently doing is the right thing or enough. In many cases, we're simply fooling ourselves. Deep down, we know which habits are producing results for us and which ones are not. It's critical to listen to the voice in our heads when it tells us this.

Have the sense and the courage to course correct to ensure the consistencies you are committed too are the ones that serve your wants and needs.

> *"But his delight is in the law of the LORD; and in his law doth he meditate day and night."*
>
> —*Psalm 1:2 (KJV)*

Today's Anchor: Habits can make you or break you, so choose wisely.

Unshakable Confidence

Education Is Essential

Filling your mind and your soul with new thoughts and ways of solving problems give you important fuel that gives you the ability to travel further. You will go to places you never thought possible as you unlock new and better ways of tackling life's challenges.

Routinely seek out others who can be teachers, mentors, and experts and who can reveal life's mysteries to you. Connect with them deeply and you'll fuel your growth as you step on the gas to go places others can only imagine.

"A wise man will hear, and will increase learning ..."

—Proverbs 1:5 (KJV)

Today's Anchor: Let education shape your response.

Building a Life That Lasts

Be Helpful in Your Relationships

One of the most important priorities in a healthy relationship is being helpful and supportive. Often, this makes a big difference in the lives of others and can push them to greater accomplishments that they might not otherwise achieve on their own.

In a similar way, be grateful when others are helpful to you. That's how relationships go to the next level.

Trust, commitment, and caring about others is a two-way street. You must give it, and you must reciprocate to maintain healthy relationships with others.

> *"But to do good and to communicate forget not: for with such sacrifices God is well pleased."*
>
> *—Hebrews 13:16 (KJV)*

Today's Anchor: Learning to be a servant is how you learn to be a leader.

Asking the Right Questions

How to Remove Frustrations

Massive gratitude removes all frustrations. If you are able to wave it as you would a magic wand it will change your mind from one that is discouraged or depressed to one that is full of hope and possibilities.

This is what also makes it possible to count your aches, pains, and setbacks as blessings. From them, you increase your knowledge and experience so that you can apply these important lessons as you move forward.

Gratitude and perspective are everything. Keep them close.

> *"O give thanks unto the LORD; for he is good; for his mercy endureth for ever."*
>
> *—1 Chronicles 16:34 (KJV)*

Today's Anchor: Gratitude is more powerful than any frustration you may experience.

What This Week Changed in Me

Comparison Is the Thief of Joy

The next time you feel less than someone else or think you want to be in another life other than your own, you are guilty of a faulty comparison.

Your life and how it plays out is meant exclusively for you. Understand that you were born into this world for God's purpose and place in the universe, not someone else's.

Accept this and be grateful for all that you have been given. It will bring you the peaceful fulfillment you deserve.

"*. . . comparing themselves among themselves, are not wise.*"

—2 Corinthians 10:12 (KJV)

Today's Anchor: Immediately stop comparing yourself to others.

Weekly Reflection:

____

____

____

____

____

____

Week 37

Staying the Course

Direct Your Energy

Make a conscious choice to create priorities each day. You may already have a sense of what they are, but to achieve maximum efficiency, reaffirm them, and focus on them then execute on them. If you must adapt, that's okay, but unless it's urgent and requires immediate attention, keep working your plan.

When you don't, it means that others are creating your priorities for you. And when you let this happen, it drains and redirects your energy in ways that serve them.

> *"Thou art my hiding place; thou shalt preserve me from trouble; thou shalt compass me about with songs of deliverance."*
>
> —*Psalm 32:7 (KJV)*

Today's Anchor: Where you apply energy is where you will go.

Strength Through the Struggle

Reasons or Results

Only we know if we've done everything we can to get the results we want. However, that all changes when the results become known in the world. Then the amount of our effort becomes obvious to everyone.

You don't fail if you work relentlessly on tasks. You only fail when you hold back or never get started in the first place. Placing blame on factors and influences outside your control serve no purpose. Instead, it's much better to focus on what we can control, and apply maximum effort in those areas.

Reasons or results. You can't have them both.

> *"The slothful man saith, There is a lion in the way; a lion is in the streets."*
>
> *—Proverbs 26:13 (KJV)*

Today's Anchor: No explanation, just execution.

Winning the Ordinary Days

Good Habits Are an Important Foundation

More than any other tools you use, habits are the biggest variable that will affect your level of success.

Habits are tricky. They come in all shapes and sizes, good and bad. Those that once served you well may no longer do so. In many cases, as you outgrow certain habits, the key question to ask is if good ones have become bad because they limit you instead of propelling you.

You must audit your habits by deciding if a current habit positively affects you, others, and your goals. Use those that serve you best, and remain consistent in your efforts but flexible in your approach.

> *"LORD, make me to know mine end, and the measure of my days, what it is: that I may know how frail I am."*
>
> *—Psalm 39:4 (KJV)*

Today's Anchor: Good habits are a gift you give yourself.

Unshakable Confidence

Focus on the Process

Having faith in your process is part of the discipline required to do hard things. A quality process eliminates fear and unclear direction. Knowing with certainty what you need to do next eliminates wasted time, money, and effort.

Do not allow a negative bias on previous failed processes derail your current efforts. They are there to teach you a lesson about how to attack the future. You can use them to your advantage when you have an honest approach. This makes it easier to keep evolving.

> "*So then neither is he that planteth any thing . . . but God that giveth the increase.*"
>
> —*1 Corinthians 3:7 (KJV)*

Today's Anchor: The quality of your process determines the quality of your outcomes.

Building a Life That Lasts

Finishing Strong Is an Important Part of Integrity

You must use high levels of intention to help finish any task with integrity. Easing up and cruising into the finish line is not done in the same spirit as when you were first inspired by it.

Set a standard for yourself and an example for others by continually attacking a problem until it is resolved to your satisfaction.

It's also important to use integrity as a compass to get us back on track if we find ourselves off course. Doing so also demonstrates a high degree of character that inspires others and gives you the energy you need to finish strong.

> *"I have fought a good fight, I have finished my course, I have kept the faith:"*
>
> *—2 Timothy 4:7 (KJV)*

Today's Anchor: Do what you say you will do in all situations.

Asking the Right Questions

Do Not Let Your Yesterdays Hold You Back

Yesterday has come and gone and there's nothing you can do to change that. Dwelling on the stresses of yesterday holds you back from what comes next. Allowing anxious thoughts of what could be disrupts the focus on what needs to be done, providing no value in actually solving the issues at hand.

Attack each day in the moment. Focus on the now instead of beating yourself up over the past or worrying incessantly about the future. Both influence how you act, but you must keep them in line as part of a balanced approach that enables you to do your best work and solve your biggest problems.

"Give us day by day our daily bread."

—Luke 11:3 (KJV)

Today's Anchor: Stop living in the past. It's over and you must move on.

What This Week Changed in Me

What Is Your God-Given Superpower?

God gifts each of us with superpowers. This doesn't mean we can leap tall buildings in a single bound, turn invisible, or have superhuman strength.

It means we have worldly gifts that we can use in the service of others as God intended. This might be compassion, a strong moral code, a relentless work ethic, understanding, or other traits.

After you discover and refine your superpowers, it's up to you to consistently put them to good use to raise up your life and the lives of others.

They are a gift given to you by God for a reason.

> *"Every good gift and every perfect gift is from above, and cometh down from the Father of lights ..."*
>
> *—James 1:17 (KJV)*

Today's Anchor: Pick one behavior that honors your superpower and lean into it as hard as you can.

Weekly Reflection:

____

____

____

____

____

____

Week 38

Staying the Course

Letting Go Is the Path to Peace

When you learn to let go of the things you can't control, you are well on your way to a path of peace. We sometimes find this to be difficult because it's in our nature to want to control everything in hopes of enjoying an outcome we want.

Doing this comes at the cost of angst, anxiety, lack of sleep, and the feeling of failure. Ironically, this is opposite of the success we are striving for. It's also ironic that letting go requires self control.

Stop trying to always steer a car God is driving. Instead sit back and enjoy the conversation, the music, and the ride, and you'll arrive at the destination He has chosen for you.

> *"The LORD will give strength unto his people; the LORD will bless his people with peace."*
>
> *—Psalm 29:11 (KJV)*

Today's Anchor: Letting go enables you to choose a better path that God has chosen for you.

Strength Through the Struggle

Don't Let Fear Paralyze You

Fear can propel you or paralyze you. It takes courage to bravely push through the thoughts and challenges that hold you back from what makes you great.

Rise to the moments that scare you and do it with confidence. Do so will push away the fear of starting, making mistakes, or failure.

Confidence builds momentum while removing the imaginary limitations in your head. It is the fuel that overcomes fear when you let it.

> *"What time I am afraid, I will trust in thee. In God I will praise his word . . . what can flesh do unto me?"*
>
> *—Psalm 56:3–4 (KJV)*

Today's Anchor: Analysis paralysis kills momentum and keeps you stuck in places you'd rather not be.

Winning the Ordinary Days

The Importance of Consistency in Teams

For maximum efficiency and results, it's imperative that all members of the team you lead are on the same page. They must be clear on their purpose, the roles they play, and results they're expected to produce.

This requires alignment and clear communications on you as the leader. You must also be flexible within the framework on the overall goal you want the team to achieve to produce winning results.

> *"Fulfil ye my joy, that ye be likeminded, having the same love, being of one accord, of one mind."*
>
> *—Philippians 2:2 (KJV)*

Today's Anchor: Teams win when everyone pulls the same direction.

Unshakable Confidence

Growing Confidence Through Completion

Confidence is built by seeing hard things and working through them to completion.

When we do something that we thought was not possible it changes our minds about what we're capable of. Our confidence grows, even when the outcomes are not perfect because we have revealed hidden qualities about who we are.

The higher the degree of difficulty in things we attempt, the greater the rewards we'll experience when we accomplish them. We become more convicted about who we are and how we're growing into the person we want to be.

> *"When Jesus therefore had received the vinegar, he said, It is finished: and he bowed his head, and gave up the ghost."*
>
> *—John 19:30 (KJV)*

Today's Anchor: You're not judged by what you start, but by what you finish.

Building a Life That Lasts

Mastery and Moving Forward

Mastering a skill or completing a task produces growth that moves your life forward in new and exciting ways.

To achieve mastery requires time, patience, and repetitive practice until there are no doubts in your abilities. This breeds confidence that you can move forward to bigger and more challenging ways.

It is humbling to dive into the darkness of the unknown, but that is where your biggest adventures wait, especially after you master the skills you need to shine the light where that darkness no longer exists.

> *"Whoso keepeth the fig tree shall eat the fruit thereof: so he that waiteth on his master shall be honoured."*
>
> *—Proverbs 27:18 (KJV)*

Today's Anchor: The highest form of success comes from practicing until you master a skill that you can use for the rest of your life.

Asking the Right Questions

Why Are We More Forgiving of Our Friends?

Do you fall into the trap of being more forgiving of your friends than yourself?

Instead, we should be kinder to ourselves. Be careful what you say to yourself because you're always listening.

If you don't like what you hear, change the message because we must give ourselves the same grace as we give others.

"*. . . thou wilt cast all their sins into the depths of the sea.*"

—*Micah 7:19 (KJV)*

Today's Anchor: Treat yourself with grace.

What This Week Changed in Me

Each Day Is Not Promised

Too often we are rudely reminded of how abruptly things can end without notice in ways that are unsettling. As we grow older, we learn this tough lesson and it humbles us and we gain wisdom when we experience unexpected pain.

This is also part of what fuels us with a sense of urgency as we gain insights on the fragile nature of daily life. We should use these instances to remind ourselves of the gifts we have been given, including the joy of living each day.

> *"Man is like to vanity: his days are as a shadow that passeth away."*
>
> *—Psalm 144:4 (KJV)*

Today's Anchor: Live each day fully because you never know how many more you will get.

Weekly Reflection:

____

____

____

____

____

____

Week 39

Staying the Course

The Power of Unconventional Wisdom

Conventional wisdom is often accepted as fact and isn't usually questioned. However, unconventional wisdom, although it is often challenged, can be the most impactful.

Questioning previously accepted truths can be eye-opening in all areas of your life. It can take time, and you may need to be patient as you find new ways of solving problems and advancing projects with satisfying payoffs as a result.

Is it time to think outside of the box to find new and unconventional ways to move the needle?

"If any of you lack wisdom, let him ask of God ..."

—James 1:5 (KJV)

Today's Anchor: Thinking outside the box is how new pathways are made.

Strength Through the Struggle

Reframing Negative Thoughts

A lifelong association with a limiting belief is not easy to part with, but with a strong-willed effort and determination we can erase them.

Start by understanding that limiting beliefs were planted by others in pain. Once we know the source of that pain, we can focus our efforts and move through that pain head on or we can replace the pain with a more positive mindset.

Until you remove these types of barriers, you will struggle to reframe your life and follow your new mindset to infinite growth opportunities.

> *"In the multitude of my thoughts within me thy comforts delight my soul."*
>
> *—Psalm 94:19 (KJV)*

Today's Anchor: Anchor yourself in reframing your thoughts and let the rest fall into place.

Winning the Ordinary Days

Fall in Love with the Process

Staying the course when pulled in many directions is the difference whether something is optional or mandatory. We want mandatory success and results, but we treat the actions to get there as optional, wondering why the end result isn't what we had hoped.

Only when we realize our actions must meet our ambitions can we see the endless path of results we desire. Falling in love with the process, regardless of the process, is how we fall in love with the results we desire.

> *"Serve the LORD with gladness: come before his presence with singing."*
>
> *—Psalm 100:2 (KJV)*

Today's Anchor: Creating a great process is the first step to the process itself.

Unshakable Confidence

Instant Implementation

The key to momentum is instant implementation. Procrastinating makes no sense due to the fear of failure or lack of time. You must lead yourself through limiting beliefs to create your best possible outcomes as quickly as you can.

Understand that you only truly fail when you lack the implementation of something you desire. The worst outcome of inaction is that you'll learn nothing new and become more frustrated by your lack of common sense and courage to make your life better.

> *"Say not unto thy neighbour, Go, and come again, and to morrow I will give; when thou hast it by thee."*
>
> —*Proverbs 3:28 (KJV)*

Today's Anchor: What are you waiting for? Your competition?

Building a Life That Lasts

Awareness in the Present Moment

Remaining present and savoring moments as they happen takes discipline. Too often, we are so busy and fixated on what comes next to fully enjoy what is taking place now. That robs us of the joy that God has put into our lives and the gifts He has bestowed on us.

Instead of immediately moving from one moment to the next without reflection, enjoy what you have been given before moving on to the anticipation of upcoming greatness. If you don't, you'll miss the greatness that is happening to you now.

"Give us this day our daily bread."

—*Matthew 6:11 (KJV)*

Today's Anchor: Do your best to focus on the here and now as often as you can.

Asking the Right Questions

Conflict or Compromise?

When we're threatened, our natural response is protecting ourselves by any means possible. We can become defensive, leading to greater conflict, or we can lead with grace, often finding a path that is lighter and clearer.

Grace is a powerful tool when used correctly. Use it to lessen conflict and find compromise when you can.

> *"God is my salvation; I will trust, and not be afraid."*
>
> *—Isaiah 12:2 (KJV)*

Today's Anchor: Let conflict or compromise pull you forward instead of pushing you back.

What This Week Changed in Me

The Importance of Candor

It's important to tell the people you lead what they need to hear versus what they want to hear. Delivering difficult messages isn't easy, but you must be honest, even when the news is bad, to build trust.

Candor is the medicine that helps an entire team pivot and course correct to better ways of moving things going forward. Be clear and concise to create a narrow focus and to dispel rumors that may undermine what you want to accomplish.

Align wants and needs so that actions meet ambitions and purpose is consistent across all levels of your team.

> ". . . *Speak ye every man the truth to his neighbour; execute the judgment of truth and peace in your gates:*"
>
> —*Zechariah 8:16 (KJV)*

Today's Anchor: Be honest, even when it doesn't serve your best interests.

Weekly Reflection:

____

____

____

____

____

____

Week 40

Staying the Course

Perseverance and Preparation

Looking for the blind spots in your ventures will minimize mistakes and accidents you'll encounter.

Most people believe that leaders, entrepreneurs, and visionaries roll with the punches. But that's because they have prepared for setbacks. They have established alternatives and ways to counter unknown circumstances and setbacks until they can regain control again.

Preparation is one part perseverance and one part confidence. It's understanding you can hit a home run on every pitch, but you can practice for every type of pitch that is thrown at you and take your best swing to get the hits you want.

> *"He giveth power to the faint; and to them that have no might he increaseth strength."*
>
> *—Isaiah 40:29 (KJV)*

Today's Anchor: Anticipate the hit before it comes. Prepare now so you don't panic later.

Strength Through the Struggle

The Problem with Expectations

Expectations are often overlooked as a piece of our life that fuels our frustrations.

What expectations in our life are misaligned with reality? What expectations have we set for others that are misaligned?

When expectations are set without proper alignment it creates frustration and disappointment not only for others but also for ourselves. Recalibrating those expectations are how we serve others and ourselves with integrity while avoiding anger and resentment.

> *"Fear not: for I have redeemed thee, I have called thee by thy name; thou art mine."*
>
> *—Isaiah 43:1 (KJV)*

Today's Anchor: Recalibrate the story you're telling yourself; alignment kills frustration.

Winning the Ordinary Days

Embrace Good Habits

More than any other tools you use, habits are the biggest variable that will influence your level of success.

When you make a shift from poor habits to good ones, you build confidence and momentum. The key is to make the change and then remain consistent long enough to turn new habits into your new normal.

> *"That ye put off concerning the former conversation the old man, which is corrupt according to the deceitful lusts;"*
>
> *—Ephesians 4:22 (KJV)*

Today's Anchor: Audit what you repeat. Small habits decide big outcomes.

Unshakable Confidence

Maintaining Focus

Maintaining focus when life is attempting to knock you off course is your choice. While circumstances may make that more difficult, if your purpose is true and the prize is enough, you must find the resources to overcome barriers in your way.

Having confidence in what you want to accomplish is an incredible defense against inevitable setbacks that stand between you and getting what you want. Ignore these attempts to send you backwards. Use confidence to stay diligent and keep moving forward.

> *"Turn away mine eyes from beholding vanity; and quicken thou me in thy way."*
>
> *—Psalm 119:37 (KJV)*

Today's Anchor: Keep your eyes on the target—noise doesn't get a vote today.

Building a Life That Lasts

The Power of Forgiving Yourself

When you make mistakes do you take it out on yourself too much? Many people do, instead of forgiving themselves as a necessary and positive step forward. It's important to reflect on our actions, but we must limit this exercise and quickly turn our attention to pour our energy into what we need, and what others need, to grow from it.

Remove the anchors of your past and instead look how far you have already come. Don't needlessly weigh yourself down. This will enable you to move through the present much easier along a path that destiny has placed in front of you.

> *"If we confess our sins, he is faithful and just to forgive us our sins, and to cleanse us from all unrighteousness."*
>
> *—1 John 1:9 (KJV)*

Today's Anchor: Drop the weight, learn the lesson, and move forward lighter.

Asking the Right Questions

When You're Challenged Under Pressure

The true test to determine if you can maintain new habits is how well you implement them in pressure-filled situations. When these habits are integrated into what you're doing, this is an indicator they will become a permanent part of your processes.

New habits are easier to consistently use under controlled circumstances. We can maintain our composure when a routine has been established. But until we test those habits in times of chaos, we're not completely sure we've done enough work to optimize them.

> *"Therefore all things whatsoever ye would that men should do to you, do ye even so to them: for this is the law and the prophets."*
>
> —*Matthew 7:12 (KJV)*

Today's Anchor: Pressure reveals what's real. Protect your standard when it gets messy.

What This Week Changed in Me

Remaining Humble in Your Heart

Remain humble in your heart, always giving thanks for every situation life gives you, good and bad.

This is especially important in your relationships with others. Those who inspire, love, and make you a better version of yourself are precious in many ways. They are part of your journey and will help you accomplish the worthwhile things in life you want most. It is not a solo effort.

Staying humble is part of an abundance mindset. Moving in this direction is critical to removing fear and scarcity that others have tried to plant in us over time.

> "*. . . be clothed with humility: for God resisteth the proud, and giveth grace to the humble.*"
>
> *—1 Peter 5:5 (KJV)*

Today's Anchor: Stay grateful and grounded; humility keeps abundance flowing.

Weekly Reflection:

____

____

____

____

____

____

Week 41

Staying the Course

Refuse to Be a Victim

You have that choice. We can accept what is happening and use it for the good of growth, or grovel by blaming others to divert from our shortcomings.

Lessons are constant, but how long we take to learn them is up to us.

> *"Be not overcome of evil, but overcome evil with good."*
>
> —*Romans 12:21 (KJV)*

Today's Anchor: Choosing to be a victim puts you at a disadvantage in ways you can't see but others can.

Strength Through the Struggle

Falling into the Trap of Complacency

Complacency is the death of growth. When we live off of our past accomplishments instead of looking forward to new challenges, we can fail in an important quest to keep growing.

You must focus on moving forward through difficulties, challenging yourself to do new things.

This sets us apart from others who don't take on challenges because they're comfortable. They are denying themselves a better future.

Action and progress separates those who say they want more from those who consistently attain it.

"Not slothful in business; fervent in spirit; serving the Lord;"

—Romans 12:11 (KJV)

Today's Anchor: Comfort is a sneaky thief; stay hungry and keep growing.

Winning the Ordinary Days

Action Is the Key

Creating ambitious goals is admirable but you won't succeed unless you actively engage in activities that move you closer to those goals. It's one thing to think about what you want to do, but action is the key that unlocks results.

The only way to overcome these feelings is to execute on our goals by moving forward and pushing through mental barriers that are holding you back.

> *"But be ye doers of the word, and not hearers only, deceiving your own selves."*
>
> —*James 1:22 (KJV)*

Today's Anchor: Motion creates momentum. Start before you feel ready.

Unshakable Confidence

Keep Track of Your Strengths and Assets

You will engage in challenges that will test you. Before you enter into these battles, you must take stock and account for all the good things in your life. This form of gratitude will also have the effect of making you stronger when people and circumstances come at you hard.

Take time to take stock. Do it as often as you need to boost yourself up for what's to come. This will remove fear and lead you to a light that lets you see during dark times.

> *"Be thou diligent to know the state of thy flocks, and look well to thy herds."*
>
> *—Proverbs 27:23 (KJV)*

Today's Anchor: Know what you have, steward it well, and build from strength.

Building a Life That Lasts

The Power of Resilience

Resilience is a critical tool to call on when we are at our lowest energy point. It helps us stay focused and give our best efforts when we are at pivotal points in our journey.

Pull from your valuable experiences and find the lessons you learned to better position you for the challenges you face now or in the future.

> *"We are troubled on every side, yet not distressed; we are perplexed, but not in despair;"*
>
> *—2 Corinthians 4:8 (KJV)*

Today's Anchor: You can bend without breaking when you keep your heart steady under pressure.

Asking the Right Questions

Stop Drifting Off Course

We can lose focus or our attention pulls us in directions that don't align with our goals. It's easy to drift instead of maintaining a steady direction, and when we do this over time, we can make the problem worse.

If this happens and we're at risk of complete detachment, we must seek counsel from our inner circle. Their mentorship can save valuable time and effort, putting us back on track quickly. We must also use the anchors of reason and purpose to remind us of what are the most important things in our lives. Without these anchors firmly in place, we are at risk of drifting off course more easily.

> *"Therefore we ought to give the more earnest heed . . . lest at any time we should let them slip."*
>
> *—Hebrews 2:1 (KJV)*

Today's Anchor: Small drifts become big detours so realign before you're lost.

What This Week Changed in Me

Honoring Your Commitments

We have the option every day to show up big or hang it up before we start. For rest or resilience. To stay focused or be distracted. To do the hard work or the easy tasks.

Don't do it for others. Do it for yourself. Part of creating the best version of yourself doesn't always involve winning. Sometimes the most difficult thing we can do is commit to starting and staying on track to prove something to ourselves.

Committing to a goal is a stepping stone to greatness. See your commitments through to the end. Keep at it until you reach the end. You can build on any outcome when you refuse to give up, earning self-respect and the respect of others along the way.

> *"When thou vowest a vow unto God, defer not to pay it . . . pay that which thou hast vowed."*
>
> —*Ecclesiastes 5:4 (KJV)*

Today's Anchor: Keep the word you gave when it was easy to promise.

Weekly Reflection:

____

____

____

____

____

____

Week 42

Staying the Course

Finishing Is the Hardest Part

We're judged by what we finish, not by what we start. Many people get hung up on crossing the finish line because they are worried that once they do, they'll be scrutinized for the outcome. They risk criticism, lower self-esteem, and other external negative noise that can be hard to accept.

Focused people know that when we're worried, tired, insecure, frustrated, and don't see the end in sight is when we need to pick up the pace. Whatever it is, likely it isn't the hardest thing you have ever done or will have to do. However, if it is, you should be excited at growing your life to a new level you've never been to before.

Crossing that finish line is a transformational step that you won't be able to fully understand until it's completed. Completion is the only way toward enlightenment, despite any doubts we may have.

Finish strong.

"Be thou faithful unto death, and I will give thee a crown of life."

—Revelation 2:10 (KJV)

Today's Anchor: Finishing is faithfulness to a process when it's inconvenient.

Strength Through the Struggle

The Difference Between Optional and Mandatory

When you struggle with staying on course, you must make choices to protect your time and resources. The simple way to do this is to decide if the steps you want to take to advance your mission are optional or mandatory.

Falling in love with the process, regardless of what it is, is how we fall in love with the results we desire.

> *"He that is faithful in that which is least is faithful also in much . . ."*
>
> *—Luke 16:10 (KJV)*

Today's Anchor: Treat the small things like they matter, because they shape who you become.

Winning the Ordinary Days

Stay True to Your Purpose

You are wise to remember often who you are and what you want to do in life.

This is a critical reinforcement tool that you must use because there are many forces in the world that oppose you and will whisper negative and distracting paths. Don't listen to them!

Instead, silence your limiting beliefs by revisiting your core purpose and reminding yourself of the gifts God has bestowed on you. Ignore all naysayers, especially the voices inside of you. Keep your life pointed in the right direction by only allowing the right thoughts in.

> *"Who hath saved us . . . according to his own purpose and grace . . ."*
>
> *—2 Timothy 1:9 (KJV)*

Today's Anchor: Your purpose gets louder when your priorities get cleaner.

Unshakable Confidence

Staying in the Present Moment

If you're in an extended battle, the key to victory is focusing on today. When you have a well-thought-out plan, the devil is in the details, and executing those details requires your full attention every day until the outcome has been decided.

To help you, focus on gratitude, peace, execution, and energy. These keep you from looking too far forward so that you can move quickly to enact solutions that work best today.

Shiny objects in the distance take away from your daily goals. Stay grounded in today. Focus on remaining confident in what you want to do, and watch unnecessary noise fade away into the past.

> *"It is of the LORD's mercies that we are not consumed . . . They are new every morning . . ."*
>
> *—Lamentations 3:22-23 (KJV)*

Today's Anchor: Don't borrow tomorrow's problems when you have plenty of challenges today.

Building a Life That Lasts

Know Your Purpose

You were brought into this world for a purpose, not to be busy. Searching for it and truly embracing it will bring you peace in all things you do.

Purpose separates those who are productive versus going through the motions. It opens up curiosity and a desire for more knowledge instead of choosing ignorance. And it is what often separates the grateful from those who are filled with resentment.

It's up to you to discover your role, which leads to your purpose, so you don't miss out on its glory. Whatever else you've been through in the past, know that today you are worthy of the rewards meant for you when you stay in the present and close to your purpose.

> *"The LORD will perfect that which concerneth me: thy mercy, O LORD, endureth for ever: forsake not the works of thine own hands."*
>
> *—Psalm 138:8 (KJV)*

Today's Anchor: Stop chasing busy; live with intention and let purpose lead.

Asking the Right Questions

Practicing the Art of Healing

You must learn to practice healing tactics and strategies. The key word here is *practice* because it is directly linked to action. Unless you take action to fight against what's ailing you, there will be no healing, only more pain and frustration.

Take time to reflect until you know which wounds are still open the most discomfort so you can focus on healing them and move forward.

"He healeth the broken in heart, and bindeth up their wounds."

—Psalm 147:3 (KJV)

Today's Anchor: Healing is allowed today, and it's important to let God do the work you can't force.

What This Week Changed in Me

Getting Back Up

After you get knocked down, getting back up is just as important as the first step you took, especially when you challenged yourself in something new.

You must have a "no matter what" mentality to take you to any destination. If your mind is filled with excuses and a desire to give up, you will use them to undermine your efforts, they will lead you nowhere.

Remove those negative thoughts and replace them with determination to get back up. Keep going until you reach your intended goal. That's where you'll meet a new version of yourself.

"Cast down, but not destroyed."

—2 Corinthians 4:9 (KJV)

Today's Anchor: Falling isn't final when you decide to stand up with wisdom and keep going.

Weekly Reflection:

____

____

____

____

____

____

Week 43

Staying the Course

Make Diligent Decisions

Staying diligent when you meet significant opposition is hard. Distractions and barriers will try to steer you back to your former self. When you can spot these challenges early, you are better equipped to develop strategies to minimize their impact on you.

Part of this involves reaffirming your desire to stay diligent in the purpose and passion you have for your goal. Also remember to call on God. This way you can let go and He will lead you to where he wants you.

"Shew me thy ways, O LORD; teach me thy paths."

—Psalm 25:4 (KJV)

Today's Anchor: Ask for the path, then walk it one obedient step at a time.

Strength Through the Struggle

Renewal Versus Results

Balancing rest versus results matters. Integrating them into your life is important but you must be careful when to choose to do so. It is not appropriate in the heat of battle as this may cause you to lose momentum and inspiration.

Instead, rest after you accomplish your goal, big or small. Use it to recharge and set your sights on the next thing you can build on.

> *"He shall not be afraid of evil tidings: his heart is fixed, trusting in the LORD."*
>
> *—Psalm 112:7 (KJV)*

Today's Anchor: A steady heart beats through loud moments when life gets noisy.

Winning the Ordinary Days

Recommitment Is Vital

When you have been working toward a goal for a while, there can be a tendency to get frustrated when you aren't seeing the outcomes you had hoped for.

When this happens, you must stop and recommit. This is often more important than your initial commitment to what you wanted. Many people skip this step because their ego won't allow them to stop and admit they needed to change course or to dig deeper than they already have. What they don't realize is the ego is the mask of insecurity.

> *"Remember therefore from whence thou art fallen, and repent, and do the first works . . ."*
>
> *—Revelation 2:5 (KJV)*

Today's Anchor: Come back to your first priorities reset and rebuild the right way.

Unshakable Confidence

Never Give Up

Perseverance through adversity feeds the belief of who we are capable of being. When you fight through adversity, you build confidence. Giving up too soon for the wrong reasons chips it away.

Persevering is hard but the rewards are worth it. Giving up can feel hard, but it is comparatively easy to walk away from something that causes you discomfort. In the long run, it creates more doubt and can have long-lasting impacts.

Always get back up. Persevere and stay locked into your long-term goals and the reasons you took on the challenge in the first place.

> *"But we are not of them who draw back unto perdition; but of them that believe . . ."*
>
> *—Hebrews 10:39 (KJV)*

Today's Anchor: Adversity is a test that may try to drown you. Hold the line and keep believing.

Building a Life That Lasts

You Can't Control Everything

As you try to steer your life in the direction you want, you will try to manage as much as you can to ensure a great outcome. But the nature of life is that there will always be things beyond your control.

Many times, you just need to dive in and do the best you can to drive things forward. Forcing your will on things you can't control is wasted energy that will set you back instead of furthering your mission.

Adopt a mindset that includes letting go of some things so that you can focus on what you can control and what matters most. This is a powerful way to think when control is beyond our reach.

> *"For that ye ought to say, If the Lord will, we shall live, and do this, or that."*
>
> *—James 4:15 (KJV)*

Today's Anchor: Release what you can't control and commit to what you can.

Asking the Right Questions

Don't Let Others Bring You Down

You have a choice. You can either let others drag you down to their level, or you can attempt to elevate them to yours.

Some people simply refuse to live life in happy and meaningful terms. They are not playing by the same rules as you. You must hold the line and refuse to sink to whatever level they want you at. When others challenge these things or they don't align with your view of life, try not to remove yourself until you make attempts to guide them up. You might be surprised at the outcome.

However, the most important thing to remember is to stay true to your vision, and not theirs.

Whose opinion has been weighing on you more than it should, and why have you given it that power?

"The LORD is on my side; I will not fear: what can man do unto me?"

—Psalm 118:6 (KJV)

Today's Anchor: You don't need approval from others on how to keep going. All that matters is that you do.

What This Week Changed in Me

Stay Focused on Today

Mourning the loss of the past is acceptable if you are focused on the present. When all you do is look backward, you miss out on the beauty of today's potential for success and the lessons you'll learn along the way.

Soon enough, today will also fade into the past. If you want to look back on this day fondly, then pour everything you can into it. Only give the past an acknowledgment.

You are no longer the person in those circumstances and it's foolish to relive what has already been instead of what today can be.

> *"Cause me to hear thy lovingkindness in the morning . . . cause me to know the way wherein I should walk."*
>
> —*Psalm 143:8 (KJV)*

Today's Anchor: Start your day with direction, not distraction.

Weekly Reflection:

____

____

____

____

____

____

Week 44

Staying the Course

Driven by Common Purpose

When a group of people are driven by a common purpose, failure is much less likely to occur. If a task is particularly challenging, the group may experience setbacks along the way, but the power of the group's knowledge and resources can minimize these setbacks and recover purpose and direction more quickly.

Common purpose creates momentum so that no single source must do all the work. It is a shared responsibility for a common goal. Shared wins also raise the entire effort so that all can enjoy the outcome.

> *"Behold, how good and how pleasant it is for brethren to dwell together in unity!"*
>
> —*Psalm 133:1 (KJV)*

Today's Anchor: Unity multiplies strength; row in the same direction.

Strength Through the Struggle

Recommit to Passion and Intention Daily

Every day brings new opportunities and challenges to explore and conquer. Starting each day fresh is a reminder to recommit to passion and intention daily.

Your life is a series of one day journeys, each one different from the others. By focusing on passion and intention, you create a path of perseverance that steers you through the ups and downs each day brings.

Stay on the path you have been forging day after day and soon you will see results that will surprise others and validate your approach.

> *"Whether therefore ye eat, or drink, or whatsoever ye do, do all to the glory of God."*
>
> *—1 Corinthians 10:31 (KJV)*

Today's Anchor: Let your daily effort carry eternal weight.

Winning the Ordinary Days

Stop!

Stop complaining.
Stop assigning blame.
Stop overthinking things.
Stop making excuses.
Stop treating others poorly.
Stop wasting time, especially on those things that don't matter.

Understand that the only way to fix problems in your life is by taking action. Do what it takes to fix a situation and keep moving forward until you are satisfied with the results.

> *"Set a watch, O LORD, before my mouth; keep the door of my lips."*
>
> *—Psalm 141:3 (KJV)*

Today's Anchor: Pause long enough to choose your next thoughts and actions wisely.

Unshakable Confidence

Honoring Your Rearview Mirror

When we revert back to old ways of thinking that no longer serve us our initial response is to set them aside instead of taking ownership of them.

Denying them renders their lessons less useful than they could be to our present situation. We can take what the past has taught us and turn those lessons into tactics and strategies that provide greater insights and serve us better today.

Not processing past thoughts is also an invitation for them to take root in ways we don't want. Instead, sit with them and find out why they have returned to your mind. When you unlock these answers you can more fully use the wisdom they provide to help you move forward.

> *"Whoso is wise, and will observe these things, even they shall understand . . ."*
>
> —*Psalm 107:43 (KJV)*

Today's Anchor: Your past can teach you without owning you.

Building a Life That Lasts

Understanding Your True Why

Take time to understand why you want to accomplish something. When you are clear on your purpose you can fully tap into the knowledge, energy, and direction you must go to because your motives and reasoning are clear.

It may take some time to be fully engaged with your why. It doesn't matter when, only that you become laser-focused early in the process. When you do, you'll find you have planted a true seed so you can water it properly from the roots, not the surface.

This is the most effective way to make a dream into reality.

> *"For it is God which worketh in you both to will and to do of his good pleasure."*
>
> —*Philippians 2:13 (KJV)*

Today's Anchor: Check your motives, knowing that your why sets the direction of your life.

Asking the Right Questions

The Illusion of Personal Rejection

When you fail, you may be tempted to frame it as personal rejection. This type of thinking serves no purpose and is often an illusion that masks reality.

There are many reasons you don't always achieve success and few of them are directly a result of your actions. Circumstances beyond your control, others dealing with you in bad faith, or the overall structure of your approach are common reasons for failure, and not one of them should be construed as personal rejection of who you are.

Deep down, when we see who we are and know our character and what we're capable of, we create beliefs that are the opposite of rejection. These insights bolster our efforts and make us immune to the poison that can infect our minds.

> *"If the world hate you, ye know that it hated me before it hated you."*
>
> —*John 15:18 (KJV)*

Today's Anchor: Not everyone's reaction is about you. Stay secure in who you are.

What This Week Changed in Me

Don't Run from Your Challenges

Many times, we avoid obvious problems, hoping they will solve themselves or simply go away with time. Relying on fate this way rarely turns out in our favor. Instead, it's better if we face our problems while they are still manageable and solve them as quickly as possible.

Procrastination is born out of fear and ignorance. A better way to approach challenges is with faith in God, yourself, and your team. A positive mindset can be contagious and reduce the size of complexities of a challenge to make it easier to solve.

"My brethren, count it all joy when ye fall into divers temptations;"

—James 1:2 (KJV)

Today's Anchor: Don't dodge the hard parts; growth lives there.

Weekly Reflection:

____

____

____

____

____

____

Week 45

Staying the Course

When Others Resist Your Growth

Those who have known you well for some time may be resistant when they see you growing into the person you were meant to be. Your growth may concern them because it could alter your relationship with them. This is normal and should be expected as you press forward with finding your best life.

Take a stand by not caving into the opinions of others. Maintain the course of your intentions. Pray for these people to see potential in their lives and in their own time while work at fulfilling your potential in this time.

> *"And let us consider one another to provoke unto love and to good works:"*
>
> *—Hebrews 10:24 (KJV)*

Today's Anchor: Lean into the resistance because healthy pressure produces progress.

Strength Through the Struggle

Focus on Solutions

Problems are inevitable but you should not accept living with them for long.

Solutions are where you should be setting up base camp. Focusing on solving the problem starts the important process of finding many possible ways to consider before landing on the one you are looking for.

You should also consider that failed solutions for one problem may be the right answer for another. This is why it's important to push several options. Stack as many solutions as you can.

As you retool and create new visions for the future, make sure this process is part of your standard way of seeking for success.

> *"Call unto me, and I will answer thee, and shew thee great and mighty things . . ."*
>
> —*Jeremiah 33:3 (KJV)*

Today's Anchor: Stop avoiding problems and instead ask God for wisdom that moves toward solutions.

Winning the Ordinary Days

Managing Overwhelming Emotions

When you are overcome by intense emotions, you can make poor choices that can turn a situation from good to bad, and bad to worse. To avoid this, stay grounded in discipline.

Discipline is what counters raw and unvetted thinking that can undermine solutions. Discipline removes the power of negative emotions and replaces them with facts and a path forward.

Use daily disciplines to regain balance in your life, putting your mental, physical, and emotions states in sync.

> *"From the end of the earth will I cry unto thee . . . lead me to the rock that is higher than I."*
>
> *—Psalm 61:2 (KJV)*

Today's Anchor: Let the emotions pass through instead of taking you over.

Unshakable Confidence

Letting Go of the Fear of Failure

It can be difficult to let go of the fear of failure and disappointment. We often beat ourselves up when we fall short. Instead, when we understand failure is an important part of the process, we can use what we learn to propel us to greatness in our quest to succeed.

The only type of fear of failure we should be concerned with is the failure to attempt something in the first place. If we fail to engage from the start, we are assured that our fears of failure will become a reality.

When we realize that this fear is holding us back from our best life, we need to dig deep and find the courage to push forward and get the results we want.

> *"God is our refuge and strength, a very present help in trouble."*
>
> *—Psalm 46:1 (KJV)*

Today's Anchor: Fear doesn't get the final word. God is your voice when you need help under pressure.

Building a Life That Lasts

Limit Uncertainty in Your Life

There will be times you will feel uncomfortable until you have more information. That's normal. But what isn't normal is allowing this thinking to be a permanent part of the way you live.

Ask questions, but make sure they have a purpose that advances you closer to your goals. Use questions to learn or pivot to a more effective process with a better outcome that does not paralyze you.

What you may discover is that the answers are more simple than you imagined. When you have more answers, you no longer worry about moving in the wrong direction. Your confidence level rises by limiting uncertainty. That is an important fact to remember as you reaffirm your commitment to where you want to go.

"Let all things be done decently and in order."

—1 Corinthians 14:40 (KJV)

Today's Anchor: Reduce confusion by choosing order, preparation, and clear next steps.

Asking the Right Questions

Walk in Faith, Not Fear

Sometimes we lie to ourselves about things that haven't happened, but the anxiety we create is real.

In a world where there are so many things competing with our attention with fear, we must lean into faith and gratitude to pull us out of the falsehood that holds us back.

Today chose faith that something good will happen in the future, instead of generating angst that is created out of fear that something bad will happen instead. Be the driver of your thoughts, not the passenger.

Where have I been letting fear lead me instead of faith?

> *"In God I have put my trust; I will not fear what flesh can do unto me."*
>
> —*Psalm 56:4 (KJV)*

Today's Anchor: Faith is a decision you make before the outcome shows up.

What This Week Changed in Me

Pitfalls Don't Define Us

When we reach a pitfall, we may suffer a temporary setback, but we should not let that define us. Pitfalls are necessary to guide us to where we really want to go.

They challenge us to reaffirm our commitment to our goals and to adjust and place us on the best path forward. Each time one pops up, frame it the right way. Use is as a form of light that will guide you from the darkness that the setback only first appears to be.

> *"There is therefore now no condemnation to them which are in Christ Jesus . . ."*
>
> *—Romans 8:1 (KJV)*

Today's Anchor: Your worst moment doesn't get to name you unless you let it.

Weekly Reflection:

____

____

____

____

____

____

Week 46

Staying the Course

Showing Up as the Real You

When you remove masks and filters, you create the opportunity for people to see you as you really are. Showing up as the real you inspires truth and authenticity in others. They will appreciate your transparency and will reveal who they are as well. This is how you build trust and form long-lasting relationships.

Show up as the person who God and your experiences to this point have made you to be. Be confident and build on that, knowing you are enough and essential to God's plan in lifting each other up the mountain.

> *"God is a Spirit: and they that worship him must worship him in spirit and in truth."*
>
> *—John 4:24 (KJV)*

Today's Anchor: God sees what people can't so it's important to be true to yourself.

Strength Through the Struggle

Loyalty Versus Commodity

When you build relationships, you build loyalty. This will get you through difficult times when competition is intense and your business is challenged.

Ideally, you want to keep doing business with people where there is collaboration. It's easier to have a healthy and financially secure business this way instead of being one of many.

Build loyalty by investing time, resources, and a personal connection when possible. Help people see the big picture and how they benefit best by working with you. Create answers to questions and align your energy to service the needs of others.

Anyone can be a commodity, but a successful businessperson must put in the work to build enduring loyalty.

> *"Greater love hath no man than this, that a man lay down his life for his friends."*
>
> *—John 15:13 (KJV)*

Today's Anchor: Loyalty is love with legs. Be the kind of person who attracts loyalty from others.

Winning the Ordinary Days

Starting Strong

Many races are won before they're even run. Train and prepare diligently before you step to the starting line. Don't get weighed down by past results or make excuses for imperfections as you prepare.

Consistency also requires aggressive patience by letting things play out while still closely monitoring them.

A team that stacks daily wins while plowing through adversity will produce results only reserved for champions.

> *"Wherefore gird up the loins of your mind, be sober, and hope to the end . . ."*
>
> *—1 Peter 1:13 (KJV)*

Today's Anchor: A strong start come from disciplined and intentional thinking.

Unshakable Confidence

Focused Alignment

When a team is singularly focused and in agreement in the same outcome for the same reasons they can do just about anything they set their mind to. However, when there is dissent or a lack of unity, it can build barriers that create a vacuum for progress and the joy that once surrounded it.

When you sense a team is not aligned, be vocal about it. Take steps to correct the misalignment as soon as possible to save time and disagreements. Do this as quickly as possible so you can collectively regain focus.

Where you focus as one, it expands efforts and increases chances for success. When you lose that alignment, you run a greater risk of a less than optimal outcome.

> *"Endeavouring to keep the unity of the Spirit in the bond of peace."*
>
> *—Ephesians 4:3 (KJV)*

Today's Anchor: Alignment isn't accidental. It is the product of intentional thinking.

Building a Life That Lasts

Transparent Trust

Authenticity in your purpose will always rise and show itself to the world. People can spot someone who is less so, and their guard will be up.

You must always be clear and confident when you display your authenticity. Approach your interactions with conviction in what you believe and you will be able to communicate effectively, making it easier for people to see your point of view.

You will resonate from a position of strength and truth that give you the best chance for a great outcome.

"But let your communication be, Yea, yea; Nay, nay . . ."

—Matthew 5:37 (KJV)

Today's Anchor: Say what you mean and set proper expectations.

Asking the Right Questions

Do What You Love Daily

Doing what you love and that brings you joy enables you to go through each day lighter. Do you take the time to put yourself in this position as often as possible?

The key is to make choices that build on creating this. When you make this a priority, you will stop making excuses that direct your time and effort into tasks that take from it.

Be aware that finding joy creates important alignment with raising how we feel about ourselves and what we have to accomplish in other parts of our lives.

What brings me alive that I keep pushing aside, and why am I not making room for it?

> *"The LORD shall preserve thee from all evil: he shall preserve thy soul."*
>
> *—Psalm 121:7 (KJV)*

Today's Anchor: You will be happier and more successful doing what you love.

What This Week Changed in Me

Seeking Breakthroughs

Do not let the fear of doing something hard or new hold you back from the breakthrough it provides.

When you attempt something difficult, you will battle the tendency many have of fighting negativity and the unknown. You must set these feelings aside and focus on the outcomes of what could go right.

You won't always find breakthroughs and you may fall short of your goals, but you should remain confident that no matter what the outcome, you will learn and be able to apply those important lessons in the future.

"Then they cried unto the LORD in their trouble, and he delivered them out of their distresses."

—Psalm 107:6 (KJV)

Today's Anchor: Keep seeking and keep moving.

Weekly Reflection:

____

____

____

____

____

____

Week 47

Staying the Course

Reciprocity

What can you do today to help change the life of your family, friends, and team? You have routine and mundane tasks that often rule your day. The key is to not let those required tasks get in the way of doing something meaningful for others.

You should consider serving others as part of your core, then act with purpose and intention to make a significant impact on people as often as you can.

What you'll find is that when you're open and want to help others, they will reciprocate to help you achieve your goals, too.

"For if they fall, the one will lift up his fellow."

—Ecclesiastes 4:10 (KJV)

Today's Anchor: Serve others without an expectation that it will come back to you with the same intensity.

Strength Through the Struggle

Vulnerability Requires Confidence

Vulnerability opens doors that enable you to better relate to others. When you are guarded, you block the possibility of more meaningful relationships that can create better results.

To express vulnerability requires courage and confidence in who you are. Sharing details of your personal side isn't easy. While there is risk of rejection, many times opening up to others is not only a gift to others but also to us.

Where can you be more vulnerable? Routinely ask yourself how you can share so that you can build bridges that lead to positive outcomes.

"I can do all things through Christ which strengtheneth me."

—Philippians 4:13 (KJV)

Today's Anchor: True vulnerability can't happen without the courage of taking the first step.

Winning the Ordinary Days

Adjusting Your View

By adjusting the lenses you see things through with more confidence, you will discover doing hard things you once thought to be impossible can quickly become habits.

Finding a new level of belief from within leads you to a place where you have new insights as to what you are capable of. When you find this place, keep going. Building self-confidence is the key to unlocking important habits and high performance.

Create more of these confidence-based habits and you will build an impenetrable wall that will fight off challenges that try to undermine you and challenge you to quit.

"For we walk by faith, not by sight."

—2 Corinthians 5:7 (KJV)

Today's Anchor: Change the lens, change the outcome.

Unshakable Confidence

The Value of Helping Others

If you have capacity, you must ask yourself what you're doing to help others, is it enough, and can you do more.

Instead of making it an afterthought, proactively search for ways to help others in need. Don't simply do it when it's convenient. Make it a habit and overcome distractions and challenges to place this as a priority in your life. Keep this promise to yourself, no matter what.

> *"Withhold not good from them to whom it is due, when it is in the power of thine hand to do it."*
>
> *—Proverbs 3:27 (KJV)*

Today's Anchor: Helping others is a way to help yourself.

Building a Life That Lasts

Faith and Doing the Impossible

Faith allows us to do the impossible. If we rely on our own understanding of what we are capable of it would blind us from what we are yet to accomplish. Standing alone is especially intimidating when you are facing seemingly impossible odds.

To conquer this type of fear, call on your faith. Faith bridges gaps, giving us confidence we would not usually have on our own.

When we act using it to fuel our confidence, we're well equipped to do anything we set our mind to.

> *"With men this is impossible; but with God all things are possible."*
>
> *—Matthew 19:26 (KJV)*

Today's Anchor: Faith turns the impossible into the possible.

Asking the Right Questions

Gratitude for Everything Is Everything

How often do you take time to count your blessings?

Do you fully understand the spiritual and emotional benefits of doing this daily?

This will not only fill your cup with confidence and peace but also motivate you to share it with others.

"Do all things without murmurings and disputings."

—Philippians 2:14 (KJV)

Today's Anchor: Gratitude is contagious; spread it.

What This Week Changed in Me

Make Discipline a Central Part of Your Life

Discipline is a form of building spiritual wealth. It is easy to talk about doing all the things you don't want to do but quite another to put them into action.

You will be challenged by the things you know you need or want to do. Discipline isn't fun but it's necessary to grow into who we were meant to be. The choice of comfort or discipline is as easy as the difference between winning or losing.

"Blessed are they that hear the word of God, and keep it."

—Luke 11:28 (KJV)

Today's Anchor: Disciplined people are the most successful people.

Weekly Reflection:

____

____

____

____

____

____

Week 48

Staying the Course

Learning Leads to Greatness

Seek knowledge even if it makes you uncomfortable. It is that discomfort that produces the most growth. And where there is growth, there is wealth.

This growth will eventually lead to mastery. And mastery builds confidence and leads to greater curiosity about other things. Mastering a subject attracts others seeking the same type of knowledge, and when you partner with these people, your results and wealth will grow at an exponential rate.

> *"He that abideth in me, and I in him, the same bringeth forth much fruit."*
>
> —*John 15:5 (KJV)*

Today's Anchor: The best leaders are the wisest ones.

Strength Through the Struggle

Believe in Yourself

As fundamental as it may sound, many people lose track of who they are and in the faith of who they want to be.

It's essential to remind yourself often of the positive parts of who you are and what your purpose in life is. Combining your purpose with your gifts are foundational building blocks for fulfillment.

Don't let critics undermine your gifts and your faith in yourself. If they seek to tear you down, remove them in your thoughts and in person.

Believe in who you are and associate with others who believe in you, too.

> *"Rejoicing in hope; patient in tribulation; continuing instant in prayer."*
>
> *—Romans 12:12 (KJV)*

Today's Anchor: Believing in yourself fortifies how you are able to believe more in others.

Winning the Ordinary Days

The Nature of Perception

Perception is in the eye of the beholder. Two people can look at the same thing and interpret them in entirely different ways. Many disagreements are the result of different perceptions instead of using facts over feelings to decide what is real.

When we take time to ask questions about what others see and confirm or deny our perception, we open the door to the truth. We are building bridges of understanding instead of tearing down relationships unnecessarily.

Taking this approach enables us to learn how others think while also telling ourselves a lot about how we think.

"If it be possible . . . live peaceably with all men."

—Romans 12:18 (KJV)

Today's Anchor: Perception is dangerous if you engage in it without looking more closely at a situation.

Unshakable Confidence

Living in the Present Moment

You must remain present and aware to fully appreciate the moments that matter most. When you are so busy that good things pass you by with barely a notice, you must refocus your brain to more fully appreciate the gifts you are given each day.

These are the moments that will come together to give you the sweetest memories that you can reflect on as you grow older.

Time does not slow or rewind to allow you to capture these things the same way after they have passed. Stay in those moments as they happen and you will enjoy them as they were intended.

"They are new every morning: great is thy faithfulness."

—Lamentations 3:23 (KJV)

Today's Anchor: Stay present and keep the past and the future where they belong.

Building a Life That Lasts

Reflect in Silence

Taking time to reflect in silence will enable you to hear words of wisdom your busy day has produced on your behalf. At the end of the day, find pockets of silence and savor them. This is just as important as how quickly you move from task to task throughout the day to accomplish your goals.

Silent reflection is a counterbalance that ensures you don't miss opportunities to let wisdom sink in because of all the daily noise we encounter.

Stop and listen to your inner voice regularly. It is always working on your behalf telling you important things so that you will become wiser and more grounded.

"And after the fire a still small voice."

—1 Kings 19:12 (KJV)

Today's Anchor: Silent meditation is key to a peaceful life.

Asking the Right Questions

The Joy of Serving Others

How often are we only concerned about what we can do to contribute to our own success? Do we spend enough time trying to be helpful and useful to others?

The reality is when we focus on what we can do for others to help them succeed, we are more likely to find greater success in our own lives.

Each morning, start your day by asking what the needs of others are instead of your own, and you often find answers in the same place.

> *"For even the Son of man came not to be ministered unto, but to minister, and to give his life a ransom for many."*
>
> *—Mark 10:45 (KJV)*

Today's Anchor: Service to other is a form of love for mankind.

What This Week Changed in Me

Gratitude Lives in the Heart

Gratitude must be rooted in one's heart. It can't be rooted by convenience, happenstance, or external blessings. You must practice gratitude daily for it to be consistently anchored to your life.

Do not wait for external blessings to practice gratitude. Instead, be aware of the many blessings that are already in our lives and think of them often without the need for ongoing accomplishments to fuel your gratitude.

> *"But my God shall supply all your need according to his riches in glory by Christ Jesus."*
>
> *—Philippians 4:19 (KJV)*

Today's Anchor: Maintain gratitude as a way of life.

Weekly Reflection:

____

____

____

____

____

____

Week 49

Staying the Course

Share Your Success with Others

When you accomplish something meaningful, make sure you take the time to recognize others for their contributions and reward them generously.

Success that is shared multiplies when others reap rewards. Just like doing hard things as part of a team increases the chances for success, you should do whatever it takes to ensure your team remains loyal and ready to win again.

Keep in mind that teams that stay together become more efficient, setting the table for even bigger wins in the future. This is a perfect way to help others grow and unleash their own potential as they also pursue their best lives.

"Comfort yourselves together, and edify one another."

—1 Thessalonians 5:11 (KJV)

Today's Anchor: Success multiplies exponentially when you share it with others.

Strength Through the Struggle

Assuming the Assumptions

We unintentionally assume others know how we feel: how much they mean to us and how grateful we are for them in our lives. This assumption is why we don't always take the time to express it.

We know how it lifts our own spirits when someone expresses gratitude and love toward us, even when the relationship is established and those sentiments have been expressed many times before.

Make your feelings known. Show and tell those people often. When you are honest and heartfelt, it is always welcomed by others, no matter how many times you've said it before.

Remove all doubts and assumptions and create a new level of conviction in you and in those you care about.

> *"Judge not according to the appearance, but judge righteous judgment."*
>
> —*John 7:24 (KJV)*

Today's Anchor: Trade assumptions for truth. Ask, listen, then decide.

Winning the Ordinary Days

Letting Go of Your Past

Do you dwell too much on the past? Do you lament people who are no longer in your life? Do you get down because happier times seem to have left your life forever?

While some of this is inevitable, remember that who you were is not who you are. The past is over, and it's not coming back no matter how much you pray or beg for it to do so.

Your time is better spent on who you are now and who you can be in the future. That version of you will be different than your past. Can you accept this? If so, you're ready to move on to a peaceful place instead of looking back with regret or envy.

Looking forward with optimism and wisdom is the key to perseverance and peace.

Choose who you are today and be grateful that who you were before is behind you. Let the light of your future shine brighter than the darkness of your past.

> *"Remember ye not the former things, neither consider the things of old."*
>
> *—Isaiah 43:18 (KJV)*

Today's Anchor: Release what is behind you because your next season needs your full attention.

Unshakable Confidence

Your Vision for the Future

To receive the blessings of your desires, you must do more than pray and dwell on your vision for the future. You must do the work.

When your heart is true, you will think less of what you're doing as work and more as an investment. The blood, sweat, and tears that are an integral part of the process from doing work matter the most.

When you work this way, setbacks and the wounds of your past become smaller and smaller, overtaken by the vision leading to your new reality. Unlike others who continue to struggle with blurred vision about what is important, you will achieve your desires with clarity.

> *"Write the vision, and make it plain upon tables, that he may run that readeth it."*
>
> *—Habakkuk 2:2 (KJV)*

Today's Anchor: Having a vision of a beautiful future is one small part of making it happen in real life.

Building a Life That Lasts

Be Honest with Yourself

How often do you convince yourself that you're doing better than you are? It's normal to minimize our setbacks as we attempt to focus on the positives in our lives. But we can trust ourselves when we don't take time to reflect on the data and circumstances of a situation.

Do you have it in you to be honest with yourself? Can you see facts and circumstances for what they really are, instead of living in denial for what they are not?

When you search for and accept the truth, you open the door to embrace and apply it going forward. An honest assessment of a situation, even when those facts are less desirable, lets you cultivate a path that is realistic, instead of facing a disappointment when you leave things up to your imagination.

> *"Examine me, O LORD, and prove me; try my reins and my heart."*
>
> *—Psalm 26:2 (KJV)*

Today's Anchor: Often, the hardest person to be honest with is yourself.

Asking the Right Questions

How Will You Lighten Your Load?

To succeed, you will need to challenge some parts of how you act, what you believe, and whom you associate with. The question to think about is what must you leave behind to achieve your goals?

This is not an easy question to ask or answer but when you're honest with yourself, you know some of the things you continue to carry must be reduced or removed. Also ask yourself why you continue to carry them in the first place?

Until you accept that you must carry a lighter load that boosts your endurance and focus, you will struggle with what holds you back.

It all comes down to whether you're ready to accept that certain thoughts, habits, routines, and people must be left behind to keep you moving to where you want to go instead of staying in a place where you no longer want to be.

> *"Blessed be the Lord, who daily loadeth us with benefits, even the God of our salvation."*
>
> *—Psalm 68:19 (KJV)*

Today's Anchor: Drop what drains you and only carry what helps you finish strong.

What This Week Changed in Me

The Only Guarantee Is Now

Reminding oneself our days are numbered and pass faster than we would admit is something our world avoids, until it cannot.

The reality is when we respect this at its highest level is when we truly live each day to its fullest. This drives us to chase our dreams and love others with more intention and excitement than if we believe the next was coming with certainty.

While we pray and hope for better days ahead, the most enlightened among us understand that every day is a gift and tomorrow is not guaranteed.

"Be ready always to give an answer . . . with meekness and fear."

—1 Peter 3:15 (KJV)

Today's Anchor: Guarantees about the future are not possible.

Weekly Reflection:

____

____

____

____

____

____

Week 50

Staying the Course

Cautious Counsel

Look carefully at who you are surrounded by and the activities they represent. Do this without judgment, for we have all had moments of lapsed judgment and have not been who we desire.

Going forward, we must decide who we want to be and surround ourselves with like-minded people. Not just stand with them but actively seek their counsel and offer ours to sharpen each other's iron. This is not to abandon those who are not aligned, but to offer arm's length love in a better way than it was to us.

"Be not deceived: evil communications corrupt good manners."

—1 Corinthians 15:33 (KJV)

Today's Anchor: Be smart enough to cut loose people whose plans are to destroy yours.

Strength Through the Struggle

Assumptions Versus Reality

One cannot judge the past until the present unfolds what it really is. We make assumptions about what something means and find out we were wrong the whole time. Sometimes, we live in those assumptions for years until we truly understand.

This understanding comes when we are ready and mature enough to accept what it truly is. The best we can do is not live in it but let it stay where it was in the past until God shows us the lesson it was meant for. Then we can appreciate it, good, bad, or indifferent, for all its purpose and beauty, while not missing what's in the present.

> *"He that trusteth in his own heart is a fool: but whoso walketh wisely, he shall be delivered."*
>
> *—Proverbs 28:26 (KJV)*

Today's Anchor: Assumptions are a fool's game of choice.

Winning the Ordinary Days

Focus on Thoughts That Serve You

When our thoughts are cluttered with useless information that gets in the way of our goals, we create an unnecessary burden that only holds us back.

To avoid this, you must become an expert at filtering what is important and what isn't. Stay disciplined and focused to drown out what is not helpful.

Be aware and tactical with your thoughts. Ask yourself, "Does this serve me? Does it put me closer or farther away from what I want to accomplish?" It's not easy to drown out the useless noise, but that's exactly what you must do to advance your life.

"I will set no wicked thing before mine eyes . . ."

—Psalm 101:3 (KJV)

Today's Anchor: Think about things that elevate you instead of those that tear you down.

Unshakable Confidence

Today's Blessing

Many mornings we wake without wonder and gratitude for how we got to this point in our life. We don't stop to think if the gifts we enjoy are going to continue or if they could end at a moment's notice. The only reality is that sooner or later, we come to realize we won't always have what we have now.

Focusing on our blessings should be a morning ritual filled with wonder and gratitude. When we add in the knowledge that these gifts and our time is finite, that should intensify our desires to find and appreciate blessings as often as we can.

Make your mark on each another with this mindset and watch how much more gratitude you feel and grace you give.

> *"In the world ye shall have tribulation . . . be of good cheer; I have overcome . . ."*
>
> *—John 16:33 (KJV)*

Today's Anchor: Stop for a moment to give thanks to all the blessings in your life.

Building a Life That Lasts

What Have They Got to Lose or Gain?

The risk of failure or a group's success depends uniquely on each person and what they have to lose or gain.

We must take the time to take a step back and evaluate why people want to partner with us and determine their deepest motivations.

Too many times we jump to a conclusion based on surface-level assumptions. If we want to achieve anything big with others, we must review, recalibrate, and react on a deeper level to find meaningful success for each person in the group.

> *"Every way of a man is right in his own eyes: but the LORD pondereth the hearts."*
>
> *—Proverbs 21:2 (KJV)*

Today's Anchor: Ask what motivates others instead of what motivates you.

Asking the Right Questions

Thinking of Others

Putting the needs of others above your own is one of the most important parts of becoming spiritually and emotionally mature. It removes selfishness from your life and replaces it with love.

You will look at the world differently when you extend yourself to someone. You find peace and comfort in knowing that you lightened the load of another person.

Make these efforts without hesitation and you will experience a sense of joy that comes only from serving.

> *"As every man hath received the gift, even so minister the same one to another, as good stewards of the manifold grace of God."*
>
> *—1 Peter 4:10 (KJV)*

Today's Anchor: Share yourself without reservation. Make another person's day better and yours in the process.

What This Week Changed in Me

The Power of Our Mind

Our mind is a powerful tool that does not receive enough credit as part of the manifestation of our goals. It is the place where our goals, desires, and habits are born. It is also the tool we use to ensure what we're doing matters to us and to others we care about.

Do you engage in self-talk that helps you come closer to the life you want? Or do you allow negative thinking to weigh you down and hold you back from your best life?

Creating a positive mindset takes practice especially if you grew up in a poor environment or you've let setbacks overwhelm you. But if you want to live better, as we all do, you must attack your thinking with intention and refuse to let negative thoughts rule who you are.

Winning battles in your mind is how you win the biggest battle of all . . . living your best life.

"Let this mind be in you, which was also in Christ Jesus:"

—Philippians 2:5 (KJV)

Today's Anchor: Controlling your mind is better than it controlling you.

Weekly Reflection:

____

____

____

____

____

____

Week 51

Staying the Course

The Seeds of Wisdom

Some days you are unsure where wisdom may come to lead you in your day. You may be tired or discouraged in areas of your life and wonder how you can add value to elevate others.

When you stumble this way, remember your value was bestowed on you when you were created by God. He knows who you are and where He wants you to be in life. Ask for wisdom this way and you will discover the purpose meant just for you.

Your wisdom should combine humility and gratitude for the day with the drive to help others in need. Give those people what they need and not just what they want, and you will display wisdom that will become clearer over time.

> *"For the LORD giveth wisdom: out of his mouth cometh knowledge and understanding."*
>
> *—Proverbs 2:6 (KJV)*

Today's Anchor: Plant seeds of wisdom today in order to harvest the best days tomorrow.

Strength Through the Struggle

The Perception of Your Best

What is your best? Perception of our best isn't necessarily reality; it takes unbiased perspective, counsel, or data to tell us if we truly have given it.

Our thermostat of success will only go as high as it was previously set, cooling us down when it goes too high. I challenge you to use the measurement of counsel, data, or perspective to gauge your actual best before jumping to your own conclusions.

> *"And let the beauty of the LORD our God be upon us: and establish thou the work of our hands . . ."*
>
> *—Psalm 90:17 (KJV)*

Today's Anchor: The perception of what you are capable of should not hold you back from going beyond that limitation.

Winning the Ordinary Days

Each Moment Is Precious

To fully enjoy your life, be humble and remind yourself that every moment of the day is precious and should be lived with your full attention.

When you pay little attention to the past or focus less on the future, you will live in the present moments and enjoy them without regret.

This will be your shield against moments of tragedy and periods that would otherwise beat you down with less hope or feeling good about your life.

> *"It is better to go to the house of mourning, than to go to the house of feasting: for that is the end of all men; and the living will lay it to his heart."*
>
> *—Ecclesiastes 7:2 (KJV)*

Today's Anchor: Treat today like it matters, because it does.

Unshakable Confidence

Preparing for Performance

We know when we truly do the work, and we know when we don't. When we prepare to the best of our ability, we give ourselves the best chance for success, we risk failure when we wing it.

Despite knowing this, why do we choose to pretend otherwise? Is it ego, the fear of letting ourselves down, disappointing others, or the fear of failure?

If we focus on being honest with ourselves when we answer these questions we won't have to worry about the results. We will be prepared and do the work. We will invest the sweat equity and show we have nothing left in the tank.

In time, our results will match our efforts. When we are fully prepared, our actions will match our ambitions giving us the success we are looking for.

"Well done, thou good and faithful servant."

—Matthew 25:21 (KJV)

Today's Anchor: Preparation is a choice.

Building a Life That Lasts

Begin with Gratitude

To be inspired or to inspire others, you must fill your heart with thankfulness. It reminds you to be humble while removing limiting beliefs and anxiety that doesn't serve you.

Your mind can only focus on one or the other. Make the conscious decision to focus on gratitude and your frustrations will melt away.

Choose gratitude, reminding yourself how blessed you are each day instead of second-guessing your way to less desirable outcomes.

> *"Giving thanks always for all things unto God and the Father in the name of our Lord Jesus Christ."*
>
> *—Ephesians 5:20 (KJV)*

Today's Anchor: Practicing gratitude in the morning leads to peaceful sleep at night.

Asking the Right Questions

You Know What They Say About Assuming

To make an accurate assessment of our situation we must deal with facts, not assumptions. When facts aren't readily available, we often fill in the blanks with assumptions.

Do you live in a world of assumptions because of fear? Because they are more comfortable than the truth? Or pressured by outside influences to think and act a certain way?

Ask questions and question the people behind what you're being told. Only then can you fully appreciate whether what you believe is good, bad, or indifferent as it relates to you.

> *"A fool hath no delight in understanding, but that his heart may discover itself."*
>
> —*Proverbs 18:2 (KJV)*

Today's Anchor: Fill in as many blanks as possible to get the most accurate picture of where you are.

What This Week Changed in Me

Give Grace Freely

Our capacity to give grace is less than the constant requests we require in life.

This conflict produces a tug and pull in all areas of our life and provides some of the most difficult tests of character we deal with. The solution is simple, but not easy. The answer is we must flip our mindset and give grace freely while expecting little to no grace in return.

When we make this shift, we begin to see burdens lift so that we and others can receive what all of us desperately want.

Giving grace from our newly found endless supply is the path to peace.

> *"The discretion of a man deferreth his anger; and it is his glory to pass over a transgression."*
>
> *—Proverbs 19:11 (KJV)*

Today's Anchor: You have an unlimited supply of grace in you, should you choose to use it.

Weekly Reflection:

____

____

____

____

____

____

Week 52

Staying the Course

Gratitude and Discipline's Freedom

Negative thoughts can overtake the mind quickly. We may not even be aware that it is just a poor habit that we must break at all costs.

The best way to do this is through daily gratitude and discipline daily. Your mind will fight you if this is a change, especially if it moves you out of a comfort zone, especially a poor one. Your mind likes keeping things the way they are because they create stability and less of a perceived threat.

However, when you make a shift to more gratitude and discipline of thought, you will build confidence. This confidence spirals upward to create the performance. Eliminating limiting beliefs and negative thought patterns is a decision, one that you can make at any time, including today.

> *"Whatsoever a man soweth, that shall he also reap."*
>
> —*Galatians 6:7 (KJV)*

Today's Anchor: Practice gratitude and discipline daily.

Strength Through the Struggle

Reflection Is Not Optional

Reflection and review of how you've invested your time is required. This will ensure you take in all the wisdom from your recent thoughts and actions. It is the final step in determining how you will grow and in what direction. Without this internal analysis, you are leaving things to chance instead of locking in the full value of lessons learned.

You must be honest in this assessment, good and bad, otherwise you will work on a flawed premise in the future instead of pinpointing how to use what you've discovered to your advantage.

> *"Examine yourselves, whether ye be in the faith; prove your own selves. Know ye not your own selves, how that Jesus Christ is in you, except ye be reprobates?"*
>
> *—2 Corinthians 13:5 (KJV)*

Today's Anchor: An unexamined life is an ignorant one.

Winning the Ordinary Days

Think Before You Speak

One of the oldest pieces of wisdom that has been passed down for thousands of years is to think before you speak. While this is not new, the simple brilliance of taking a beat before you speak is one of the most effective ways you can avoid unnecessary arguments, setbacks, and making poor decisions.

Today, more than ever, you must use words sparingly and powerfully.

This can be hard when we have so much to say. However, when we listen first, we often obtain all the wisdom we need so that it is not necessary.

> *"Be ye kind one to another, tenderhearted, forgiving one another."*
>
> *—Ephesians 4:32 (KJV)*

Today's Anchor: Sometimes it's best to stay quiet instead of inserting yourself into a conflict.

Unshakable Confidence

Put Your Thoughts to Work

Dwelling on possibilities and what-if thinking too much undermines our ability to make decisions.

Our thoughts play tricks on us. And when we allow them too long of a leash, they turn into an uncomfortable reality that takes us away from where we really want to be.

Think first, but then you must act. Make the conscious effort to go forward in the direction you choose. That's how you find the best version of reality meant for you.

"Walk as children of light."

—Ephesians 5:8 (KJV)

Today's Anchor: Turn thoughts into action instead of allowing them to be pit stops.

Building a Life That Lasts

Reframing Your Work

When your work feels like a vacation and you are inspired to grind on things to find greater satisfaction, you have arrived.

Work that feels like work instead of something that inspires you requires a reset. Remove the illusion of difficulty and you'll discover the joy of positive results that were there for you the entire time.

> *"For thou shalt eat the labour of thine hands: happy shalt thou be, and it shall be well with thee."*
>
> *—Psalm 128:2 (KJV)*

Today's Anchor: Attitude is one of the choices we have in our work.

Asking the Right Questions

Halftime

Think of everything you've accomplished to this point as the halftime of your life. You can't change previous results. You can only focus on the second half as you work toward the end of the game.

You have a choice when you hit this fork in the road. You can slide easily into the second half and let the results fall where they may, or you can fully attack what's in front of you like it's the beginning of the game.

You can have a big say in the outcome of the game, but you must play to win, not just to avoid the loss.

What needs to change in the second half so I do not repeat what held me back in the first?

> *"Know ye not that they which run in a race run all, but one receiveth the prize? So run, that ye may obtain."*
>
> *—1 Corinthians 9:24 (KJV)*

Today's Anchor: Recommit to your goals at halftime.

What This Week Changed in Me

Connecting to Your Purpose

An effective way to stay connected to your purpose is by humbly asking for help when it's needed. This shows you have a solid understanding of current conditions and what you want your desired results to be.

Refusing to ask for help and standing firm when facts suggest otherwise will only bring you stubborn familiarity. If you want better results, explore the possibility of change so you can create evolved solutions based on an evolved way of thinking.

> *"For we are his workmanship, created in Christ Jesus unto good works, which God hath before ordained that we should walk in them."*
>
> *—Ephesians 2:10 (KJV)*

Today's Anchor: Ask for help as if your purpose depends on it.

Day 365: Reaching the Top

Don't Give Up Too Soon

So many give up just before they are about to reach the end. Sometimes, when we can't see the top and don't know how far away it is, we shift our thinking when the climb becomes hard.

This creates another obstacle instead of digging in and doubling our focus and efforts.

How many times have you done this in the past only to find out you were closer to the summit than you imagined?

Instead of living with regret, attempt to accurately measure how much further you must go then stay the course, keeping your blinders on until the end.

Keep stepping to new heights with focus until someone taps you on the shoulder, you look up and they say, "Congratulations, you did it!"

> *"Cast not away therefore your confidence, which hath great recompence of reward."*
>
> —*Hebrews 10:35 (KJV)*

Today's Anchor: Don't measure how far you have to go more than how far you have come.

Weekly Reflection:

____

____

____

____

____

____

Acknowledgments

No one climbs alone. *Daily Perseverance*—and the life behind it—wouldn't exist without the people who pushed, challenged, and believed in me along the way. You helped shape who I am as a leader, coach, father, husband, and man.

First and foremost, to **God**—through Christ, all things are possible. Thank You for being the source of every step and every second chance.

To **Bret Colson**—your creativity and care helped turn this idea into something real.

To **Josh Sigman**, my first coach—thank you for showing me how to scale with intention and raising my ceiling before I even knew one existed.

To **Jon Gordon**—thank you for your wisdom, insights, and mentorship.

To **Ben Newman**—your fire, accountability, and relentless standard pushed me further than you'll ever know.

I also want to recognize the contributions of **Zach Schisgal** and the team at **Wiley, Tom Ferry, Ron Leonhardt, Rory Vaden,** and **Elle Kogler, Roy Mason, Pastor John Randall, Frank DeGrazia,**

Hunter Markwardt, Brad, Woody, Greg, Sue, Jimmy, Sam, Jenn, Jenna E., Lana, Aunt Jodie, Jenna, my CrossCountry team, and my Impact Elite Coaching family—especially **Josh, Gavin, Haley, and Oleg.**

About the Author

JJ Mazzo is recognized as a coach who drives growth through perseverance, serving as an EVP at CrossCountry Mortgage—The Mazzo Group and as cofounder of Impact Elite Coaching. He is a top loan originator in Orange County, California, and has consistently ranked in the top 1% nationwide for over 10 years.

He is also a decorated entrepreneur and an eight-figure business owner, as well as the *USA Today* best-selling author of *Perseverance Principles,* which tells the story of his troubled childhood, his declaring bankruptcy at age 32, and his becoming a multimillionaire by 37. It is a powerful, personal narrative of triumph over adversity, motivating others to pursue and achieve financial independence.

JJ is also active in several charities, including First Home IQ, Children's Hospital of Orange County, and Orange County Rescue Mission, and is a contributing member of Giveback Homes, providing low-income families with new homes.

He resides in San Juan Capistrano, California, with his wife and two beautiful daughters.

TOOLS . RESOURCES . TRAINING

THE WORK CONTINUES.

Free toolkit to put this book into action.

SCAN OR VISIT

PerseverancePrinciples.com/Resources

Coaching guides • Implementation tools • Daily forms

A FAVOR FROM JJ

If you found value in Daily Perseverance, please consider leaving an honest review on Amazon. I read every one, and your feedback helps shape what I build next for you.

— JJ MAZZO

Instagram @jjmazzo_ | LinkedIn /in/jjmazzo

STAY THE COURSE